the
best
of the
worst

my TRUE story of surviving and thriving
after a traumatic brain injury

Rainmaker Publishing

First published by Rainmaker Publishing 2024

Copyright © 2024 by Emily Owen

First edition

Hardcover ISBN: 978-1-961351-15-8
Paperback ISBN: 978-1-961351-11-0

Publishing support services provided by Rainmaker Publishing
To learn more visit: www.timetogetpublished.com

the
best
of the
worst

my TRUE story of surviving and thriving

after a traumatic brain injury

emily silver owen

contents

this book is dedicated to my beloved teddy,
who saved my life in so many ways

It's like being able to hear but not being able to speak or being able to see but not being able to vocalize what you see, like having hands but not being able to touch anything. Like every time you go to take a bite of something, it's too hot. Every time you take a step, your shoelace comes untied, and every time you take a sip, it dribbles out of your mouth like one of those gag cups. Every time you set out to write something down, your pen runs out of ink. You burn everything you cook. That's what it's like to be me sometimes. You can see what you want but have no idea how to obtain it—living in limbo, always in the in-between.

I will spend the rest of my life trying to right the wrong I experienced on September 7, 2019. I don't want to play the victim. It's not an excuse. I don't want to be the chick hit by a car. I want to rise. I want to be the girl who was hit by a car and wrote an entire freaking book about it. Then, she influenced her little world to be more conscious and aware of the small things. If this injury has taught me anything, it's to never take anything for granted. You never know how long it'll last. Also, remember that things can always get better.

what it's like to be me
circa march 2021

~ em

In sharing my journey of overcoming a traumatic brain injury, I aim to uplift and support others facing similar challenges. Understanding and awareness of neurodivergent brain processing is at the heart of my mission. To ensure everyone can access my story, I'm pleased to offer a large print edition, catering to those with vision difficulties like mine.

This alternative format is designed for ease and comfort, allowing the essence of resilience, hope, and community support to shine through. If you or someone you know benefits from larger print, I encourage you to explore this edition.

Please visit Amazon to obtain the large font edition

Your engagement with this version supports our collective mission to embrace and understand diverse experiences, fostering a more inclusive community. Thank you for joining us on this important journey.

love,

em

foreword

I HAD THE HONOR OF BEING EMILY OWEN'S SPEECH-LANGUAGE pathologist at Centre for Neuro Skills (CNS), a post-acute brain injury rehabilitation clinic in Los Angeles, California. By the time she arrived at CNS, six months had passed since the date of the accident, and she was still closer to the beginning of her recovery than she was to the end. And as luck would have it, the pandemic arrived just after Em started this phase.

Regardless of the obstacles stacked against her, I quickly saw in Em the determination to do whatever it would take to get better. As she improved, her personality gleamed bigger and brighter. She openly talked about her story with staff and other patients in the program, and ultimately had the idea and fortitude to write this book. I was privy to reading very rough drafts during its inception and was so excited to hear that this is yet another undertaking that she has seen through to fruition.

Rehabilitation is an integral part of recovery for individuals with brain injuries. Obtaining the right treatment at the right time significantly improves one's outcome, but there are limited treatment options when it comes to brain injury rehabilitation. It is also worth noting that it is never too late, and that tenacity, love, and hope go a long way.

Em is a testament to what is possible to accomplish in life after brain injury. When she visited me recently, I was amazed to see and hear how she has continued to transform in the years since she was discharged from CNS, while remaining true to herself, and raw and colorful about all that she has endured. I am so proud that she once again persevered and was brave enough to bare it all in this book, in hopes that it helps even just one other individual.

Victoria Katomski

Victoria Katomski, MS, CCC-SLP
Director of Rehabilitation
CENTRE FOR NEURO SKILLS®
April 2024

author's note

telling this story
putting it into my words
helps me understand

My mom died when I was a sophomore in college. That wouldn't even be the worst trauma I would experience before I graduated. When I was 22 years old and taking the last few classes I needed in a super senior extra semester, I was walking my dog before dinner, and we were hit by a car. Teddy died and I will have a traumatic brain injury for the rest of my life.

The woman who hit us was tipsy. Our accident was around 5:30. I had just taken a picture of a local bar at 5:23. The driver was on her way home from a different bar when I regrettably crossed paths with her. It was September 7, 2019.

"Just a quick drink before I go home …" she had probably thought. Stopping to have that drink would ruin both of our lives in very different ways. For her, I know enough about the driver to know this must haunt her and will for the rest of her life. She derailed my life, paused it, and forever changed my future.

When her car hit me, she killed my late and great little dog, Teddy. My mom rescued him from one of those pop-ups in front of a TJ Maxx. An old couple gave him up because he had too much energy for them. She left him to me when she died. I was his third and final owner.

It wasn't the impact of the car hitting my body that hurt my brain. It was the moving around in my skull that my brain did when I fell to the ground. Bouncing off the car and hitting the sidewalk left me with diffused axonal shearing, which means the connecting fibers in my brain were torn within locations all over my head. It's like I had shaken baby syndrome.[1]

I will always have a damaged brain because brain injuries never fully heal. On the other hand, it is now believed that they are the only regenerative brain condition, meaning you can always improve.

The parts of my brain that tell my body what to do and how to think and move were severely damaged. For almost six months, I lived in hospitals and a nursing home. I went to rehab every day after being discharged from the hospital. For a little more than a year and a half, with the support of my family and friends, I worked harder than I knew I could to get my life back from the woman who selfishly stole everything from me.

This story you're reading isn't an unbiased one. It's my life, and I'm the one living it and then writing about it. This book is written entirely from my perspective. I know there

---

[1]	Snyder, V. S., & Hansen, L. A. (2016). A Conceptual Overview of Axonopathy in Infants and Children with Allegedly Inflicted Head Trauma. *Academic Forensic Pathology*, 6(4), 608–621. https://doi.org/10.23907/2016.058

are other perspectives, and in every single interaction I've written about, there is more than just my view. I'm not saying that mine is the most accurate or the most right, but it is the perspective I've had throughout my life, it was changed and influenced by all of my past experiences.

After my mom died in March 2017, Diana's house became my home, too. It was almost unspoken. Separately, we decided I would move there and we both knew it was meant to be. Diana was my mom's best friend for 30 years, and we were always close. Our relationship went from going out to meals and shopping to living together.

A hurricane in Puerto Rico forced Diana's parents to relocate and live with her later in 2017. Since the room I had moved into was closest to her room, they took that room. She then transformed her garage into two rooms for me and my brother, Kyle. This became the "Owen Wing" of her small house, with its own private entrance. That meant that I got my own space when I came home to continue recovering. Although I refer to her as my aunt, Diana is really my fairy godmother because she gets seemingly impossible things done.

This book was mostly written in real time. I always went back to write more in the first couple of chapters, as my life changed, as I healed. My book just kept getting longer and longer as chapters were added. Sometimes, an idea of what to write would come to me late at night when I was lying in bed, and I would write paragraphs in the notes on my phone.

I wrote the first part of this book with a lot of help from my aunt. I'm grateful for her devotion and never-ending support. I wrote this book almost every day for at least six months after I got home from rehab. The rest I wrote after

I'd finished at CNS (Centre for Neuro Skills), between my naps and endless walks around the little slice of Los Angeles where I lived with Diana and her elderly mom.

It was cathartic to write everything out. Several of the names in this book have been changed or omitted, including the name of the driver who hit me, to protect their privacy. I wrote most of this book with a mug or a jar of coffee between me and the computer. First, I dictated it, Diana typing as I spoke the sentences, both of us utterly unaware of what it would become. Where was this going? Would it ever be published? Would I end up dictating an entire book? The answer to that last question is no.

At first, I started typing with just my index fingers. Tap. Tap. Tap. Then I would type it with all my fingers on my aunt's desktop, then on my laptop in my bed. Soon I switched to a more productive space in a room we kept available for my brother's visits. Writing this book became like a journal for me—a stream of consciousness at first—where I would write about what happened that day at rehab. It's not the kind of rehab where alcoholics and drug addicts go; it's where you work on your body and mind because of some horrific trauma. My story is still being written.

Much of it on my phone. Maybe you're reading this because you're living through a traumatic brain injury (TBI) or know someone with a TBI. Perhaps you're just interested in recovery or you're working in the rehabilitation field. Whatever brought you here, welcome.

I'm excited to share my story with you.

I wrote this book's chapter names, the captions for my photos, and all of the haiku featured in lowercase letters instead of capitalizing them. These aren't mistakes.

I have always been against capitalism—more in the structural sense than formatting typed work. I used to turn in some of my papers in college all in lowercase. I think capitalism is why we're in the place we are. I don't feel the world is working very well. It's almost like we're working against ourselves. We only value making more money at whatever cost.

In college, I was an environmental studies major. I learned a lot about how capitalism was terrible. I learned all about how it was the underlying reason behind much of the evil that plagues our world. I understand that lowercase letters at the beginning of every chapter won't affect how the world runs. It is a small thing I can put out into the universe to facilitate a new worldview. I wanted this book to be all in lowercase, but conventions and writing rules exist, and I will conform to some of them.

This book was initially entitled *F*** The Lady Who Hit Me*. I will never forgive or forget, but one day I realized that this book wasn't about her. The title was funny, but it gave her too much power.

When I started writing this book, my sentences and paragraphs were short and concise. I needed cues before I could write more. How did something make me feel? Why did I do something? What next? Or I would be told how things happened, and I would put it in my own words. I wrote most of this in anger toward the woman who hit me, for upending my life and sending me into the unknown. How healed will I get?

Some days I spent an hour or two hours writing. Sometimes I only stopped writing when my aunt told me to take a break and rest.

There are two different haiku in every chapter, opening and closing each. Most of them make sense and fit with their chapter. I started working with the form of haiku in my junior year of college, but I don't remember what exactly got me started writing these perfect, 17-syllable poems. I just remember loving them and that I started writing them all the time. I wanted this book to feature only haiku I've written since my injuries happened and my recovery began, so I didn't use any of the haiku I had written before I was hurt.

When I began to write with my right hand again, I wanted to write a haiku on paper with a pen. When I was eventually able to, I checked off a huge thing from my list of skills I was determined to get back.

This book is being made available in two editions: a standard edition with a traditional font size and a Large Font Edition. I know from personal experience how hard it is for anyone with a brain injury to read smaller print, so we made the Large Font Edition to help anyone who needs help reading.

I really believe reading should be available to everyone, and it was such a relief for me to find books in larger print that I could read! I knew my book would have to have a Large Font Edition, too. For details on the Large Font Edition and the inspiration behind it, please refer to the special page included in this book.

My life is split into before and after the accident. They're entirely different, but I'm starting to emerge from the middle. For a few months, I remember I felt lost inside my own body. I didn't know how to be myself or even who I was. No amount of rehab will magically make you *you* again. I was lucky enough that my personality stayed intact. My humor, intelligence, and great taste (and my *huge modesty*) didn't leave me either. It very slowly started to come out. I very slowly started to become me again.

At first, I wouldn't smile or laugh at anyone, partially because I didn't have enough control of my face but also because I didn't know we were supposed to. For a while, I lost the ability to understand what reactions were expected or appropriate. I didn't make jokes at all, and I'm known to be pretty funny, if not hilarious. My sense of humor returned, and is one of the things I'm most glad wasn't knocked out of me.

I stayed as nice as I was before the crash, although I am admittedly a lot more self-centered because I struggle to think outside my bubble and include other people. It's not that I don't care about other people, it's just my recovery and everything that goes with it takes all of my focus and time and energy. With the energy left, I do Emily things first. They take the proverbial centerstage.

I didn't get much from my accident besides seemingly endless physical and cognitive deficits. I use it as an excuse. *Sorry, I didn't do the thing you wanted me to do; I'm recovering from a brain injury, so it isn't my fault.* I know I can't use it forever, but I will use it for as long as I possibly can. If I got anything out of this whole mess, I got a good excuse for a while.

When my brain got scrambled, my long-term memory turned to crap. I used to have a stellar memory, but post-accident, it sucks. My short-term memory is okay and it gets better every day, but for about six months—from September 2019 through February 2020—my brain wasn't locking in new memories. I do have a five-year gap of spotty, fuzzy images from the moments before I was hit until the day I wrote this paragraph. I remember some things very well, while other events, it's like they didn't happen to me. I have no memories to back them up. The Before Years. Once in a while, I'll get an unexpected memory that pops into my head. When that happens, it's as if it's always been there.

when i write poems
that's the way it all makes sense
when it's in three lines

chapter 1

i am the girl who lived

i wasn't supposed
to die when the car hit me
it wasn't my time

september 7, 2019

My journey to recovery began in an emergency room, up in Arcata, a small town in northern California, where I went to college. Their ER team was the first to give me medical attention. Well, the first after the people who stopped at the scene and the paramedics in the ambulance that transported me to the ER right after we were hit because someone called 911. I later learned that my therapist knew that someone. She held my hand until the ambulance arrived and someone else cradled my head.

The ER called my aunt an hour and a half after the accident. They had my aunt's number from when I had broken my ankle a year and a half earlier and had to go to PT in that small town; I'd listed my aunt as my emergency contact. The nurse told Diana that I had been in a severe accident. Diana explained that she and my dad were in Los Angeles, so it would take them some time to get there, but she was going to call some people in Arcata and get someone there as soon as possible. So even my unconscious self wouldn't be alone. However, unbeknownst to her, some of my friends were already there.

The nurse told my aunt that I was being transferred to the ICU in Eureka because I needed a trauma center. Eureka is the biggest town nearby, about ten minutes away from Arcata. My aunt called two best friends of mine so that I wouldn't be alone in that new place. The security guards at that hospital must have thought I was a famous person or something, based on all the people who came to visit me. It was a small town, so they were used to barely anyone coming to see someone there.

My aunt called my brother, Kyle, who lived in Sacramento at the time, because he was the family member nearest to me. My dad hopped on a flight out of LA to be with me, but his flight to San Francisco was delayed and he then still had to drive to Eureka, arriving around 6 a.m. the next morning.

My best friend since kindergarten, Sabrina, a very special soul, drove my aunt up to see me. The whole time they were driving, they didn't know if I would be alive by the time they got to Arcata. It is over a 10-hour drive north from Los Angeles.

When I arrived at the Eureka trauma center, they used the Glasgow Coma Scale (GCS) to assess my degree of consciousness.[2] The GCS looks at several factors like eye-open-

---

2   Jain, S., & Iverson, L. M. (2023, June 12). *Glasgow coma scale*. StatPearls - NCBI Bookshelf. https://ncbi.nlm.nih.gov/books/NBK513298

ing, motor skills, and verbal responses. On a low scale of three (completely unresponsive and probably fatal) to a high of 15 (responsive), I scored a nine, then regressed to a five. My score of nine indicated a moderate brain injury, on the border with severe. When a nurse later reported the score of five, in the severe range, my family was even more worried.

In the ICU, they did another CT scan, and the neurologist on call informed my aunt and my dad that the results were consistent with diffuse axonal injuries (DAI). Six days later, when I was stable enough, an MRI confirmed this diagnosis.

Doctors found hematomas in the right prefrontal cortex of my brain, right inferior frontal gyrus, right thalamus, and right medial occipital lobes. They also found multifocal areas of restricted diffusion in the frontal lobes, the selenium of the corpus callosum, thalamus regions, medial temporal lobes, and midbrain compatible with shear injury. Fortunately, there were no significant intracranial mass effects or midline shifts.

These words were terrifying to hear and for me to read about afterward. Too complicated and jargony for me to try to explain. Would I even come out of my near coma? All the doctors and nurses kept repeating that my young age was a substantial favorable factor. And now, here I am, writing this book and shattering most of the expectations anyone had for me.

A lot of people came to see me that first week. Diana, my dad, and my girlfriend came to be with me. My brother and his girlfriend came in from Sacramento and my step dad flew in from Los Angeles. Many of my friends from that small town came to see me at the hospital there. I could only squeeze people's hands while they were visiting me as I was minimally conscious through multiple hospital changes and even a flight home to Los Angeles. My legs were constantly kicking the wall and even some of my friends when they visited me, partially as an involuntary movement that could have been a reaction to pain.

The car hit us in broad daylight. I had just left my house to take Teddy on a walk before dinner. Little did I know that I would never eat the dinner I had planned to make that night. My roommate, Alicia, was going to come with us on our walk but ended up not going because she needed to do homework. I told her later that I was happy she hadn't come with us that day.

Alicia told me how she found out I had been in an accident. First, she had seen a bunch of ambulances around where I had taken my walk. She asked someone who was headed her way from the direction of all the rescue squads what had happened. They told her that a girl and a little white dog had been hit by a car. She ran home and called the closest hospital to find out where I was.

When I was stable, I was flown down south to Los Angeles from Eureka in a private jet with my dad and two nurses. I don't remember any of this, but I have seen pictures of it. We took this private jet through a nonprofit organization my aunt learned about from an intake administrator at Barlow Hospital in southern California. That woman was one of many people who stepped up and helped Diana locate the best resources and facilities for me. My insurance wouldn't cover the flight. They would only cover an ambulance ride to Redding from Arcata because that was the closest place to deal with my injuries. The flight was going to be $23,000!

When my aunt talked to the administrator at Barlow Hospital, she told her the ridiculous amount of money they were asking for. So the woman told her she knew of an organization that would possibly be able to bring the cost down.

That organization is called Angel MedFlight, an air ambulance service, and they brought it down to $8,000. Which is still a lot of money, but at least it was $15,000 less than the other group initially asked for. You can read more about Angel MedFlight in the "Resources" at the back of the book.

The first time my eyes opened for an extended period was on that flight. I don't know what I was thinking or if I could even think. I must have been confused when the first time I consistently had my eyes open, all I saw were clouds outside the window. I must've thought I'd died and gone to heaven. When I got to LA, I went to a hospital called Barlow, a respiratory hospital. Barlow was a hospital where I was in a long-term acute care unit. I was still minimally conscious this whole time. The doctors called it a near coma. My eyes were open but unseeing.

One weekend, one doctor told Diana that I might need some kind of brain surgery but needed a neurologist to read my most recent scan. It turned out that the radiologist had misread my brain CT scan and thought I had a midline shift, which would mean the fluid in my brain was causing so much pressure that it might need draining.

Diana was alone at the hospital and terribly worried. Then, after a few hours, she talked to the neurologist, who looked at my brain scan and said I didn't need surgery. Nothing requiring surgery had happened. I wouldn't have been happy if I had needed surgery and had woken up from my near coma with a shaved head or even a partially shaved head. Shaved heads are way more badass when you consciously decide to shave them.

It's challenging and emotional for me to see pictures from that time. I know it happened, and there are people close to me who remember it vividly. Seeing photos of yourself from a time you have no memory of is terrifying, but I get a sick satisfaction from hearing stories about my recent past.

I don't feel connected to the stories I hear—almost like they are about someone else. New memories weren't sticking in my brain then. I still like hearing about them because it shows how far I've come and will continue to grow. It's been hard to rationalize that version of me with my current version.

In the years since our accident, I sometimes struggle to do certain things, but at least the new me is trying. Sometimes certain things are harder for me to do now. At the Centre for Neuro Skills, they talk about "our handicaps." Honestly, I don't consider myself a disabled person, but I will still take advantage of any disability discounts!

Some things are more challenging, but I always get them done. I have no idea what my life will look like in the years to come, but no one does. All I know is I'm on the road to recovery. It's not an easy road. This journey is painfully slow. I'm doing my best under the circumstances the universe has given me.

My dad has told me that I first opened my eyes after 11 days, even though this timing has been questioned. Eleven has always been a significant number in my life. I first started noticing numbers in my first year of college. I began to pay attention to the time and the license plates I saw. I have 11 dots on all my fingers that my roommate gave me one drunken night a few years ago. Two on the middle finger of one hand because I like odd numbers more than even numbers, so it had to be 11 instead of 10.

For a long time, I thought I was born at 11:10 in the morning on April 12, but I later found out that wasn't true. My email at Humboldt State was ejo110, meaning I was the 110th person to have those initials and enroll at Humboldt State. It has always been my preferred choice of number. Maybe it was fate, decided many moons ago. Maybe it's always been my destiny to be struck by a car.

It wasn't my destiny to die that day. I know I shouldn't, but I feel I am a bit karmically protected. How many bad things can happen to one person? I hope I didn't jinx something in the universe by acknowledging that. I hope that by identifying it, I did the opposite. I hope I double-jinxed it, and they'll cancel each other out if there's anyone paying attention in the universe.

I mean, there are almost eight billion people on this planet, and that's just this planet. *How can I matter in the scheme of things?* I guess that's what religion is for. Why do people turn to a faceless god? Are they scared to be just one out of eight billion? Or one in comparison to an infinite number of beings? They're afraid not to matter.

Waking up from a coma isn't like they show it in the movies. It's not like you're fast asleep one day and talking and walking the next day. It was and is a very, frustratingly slow process. First, your eyes start to open, and then weeks later, they can be open for extended periods of time. Then, months pass before you can even think of walking and talking. Things continue to be a struggle for a while. Years even.

Even while I was unresponsive at Barlow, parts of myself revealed themselves. I wore my socks unmatched. Diana told the nurses that I always mismatched my socks, and they had to put them on that way every day. All the doctors and nurses who came into my room noticed and commented on them. They usually already knew that I liked them that way. I always mismatched my socks. I have done this since halfway through high school. I'm not sure now why I started doing this. I just know that I did it on purpose.

I continue doing it now because it's something I can control. Even when I get a new pair of socks, I match them up with another unmatched pair. I heard once that it is good luck to wear mismatched socks. Not good enough because I was still hit by a freaking car. I guess I'm just different because I was hit by a car. No, I'm different, *and* I was hit by a car.

At Barlow Hospital, the walls in my room were covered with pictures and instructions. My aunt also hung up a poem I wrote sometime during my past life, which eerily describes what was happening. It was like I knew what my fate was going to be. I called it, *The In Between.*

In the middle of
what we were and
what we will be
there are no words
to describe what we are
we haven't spoken them yet.
An open ended idea of
what we could be
we're melting into the universe
I've never been here before
the in between
we haven't yet decided

what the future holds.
Living in the question mark
Accepting whatever unfolds
Here we are — in the middle
Between what we know & what we don't

Another thing on my wall was a series of diagrams so visitors could do range-of-motion exercises with me, to keep my muscles moving and reduce my stiffness. My dad, aunt, family friends, and childhood babysitter, Karla (who came in the evenings after work), did them with me. The physical therapist only came once daily in the morning and sometimes in the afternoon, but that wasn't enough for me.

The right side of my body was completely rigid at this point. While I was still primarily non-responsive, the main person there who worked on my range of motion asked me to give her a high five. I very slowly raised my left hand and gently touched her hand that was extended toward me. That was the first time I did anything that demonstrated more than a reflex, just my free will.

I have scars all over my body from the accident and the tubes.

I very briefly had a chest tube. The internet tells me that a chest tube drains blood and other fluids from around the heart and lungs. They put the chest tube in me while I was in the emergency room. I only had it in for about a week.

I couldn't chew or swallow for months, so I had to be fed through a tube in my stomach. I needed the feeding tube.

Last but not least, I might have a scar smack dab in the middle of my throat forever. They put a trach in my throat to keep my airway open, and I didn't like it. However, it did save my life. I had the trach for about four months. I looked at it when they took it out of my neck. It was annoyingly inconspicuous. It was so small for all the good it had done for me.

When I was in the early days of my injury, I couldn't have any say on anything, so to protect my privacy until I could decide for myself what I wanted shared and with whom, my family had a very strict, no-social-media posting about me, my injuries, and the accident. They said no one could post anything about what was happening, especially when I couldn't agree. Now, everything has to be checked with me. I get the final decision if it gets publicly shared about me.

Honestly, though, a couple of my friends' parents and siblings did post to Facebook and Instagram, they even tagged me in it. I'm not sure why anyone thought that was helping me or even affecting me in any way.

I know I never chose this or ever thought in my wildest dreams that it could happen. Sometimes, when confronted with how far my life is from where I want it to be, I get understandably sad. Even in my nightmares, I never thought I would be hit by a car. I was, though, and some days, it's harder to accept. I can't even begin to understand why. Some days I, like everybody, have a shitty day. They're few and far between, they probably should be more often than they are, considering I was hit by a car.

Some days when I'm really feeling and thinking darkly, I think it would have been a lot easier for me if I had died on September 7. Maybe not for the people who love me, but if I had died along with Ted, I would never know how hard it is to heal. While simultaneously grieving. Or how frustrating it is not to be able to walk correctly. Or to forget a good portion of your life. Or to have your dominant arm and hand not working well. Or to be broken up with, amid disaster. Or to not be able to dream at night. The list of things I've lost is long and overwhelming.

One day I put on one of my inherited coats and reached in the pocket. I was wearing a jacket that used to be my mom's, and I found a forgotten green poop bag that had been for Teddy. I don't want this to be who I am. I know it doesn't define me. I'm not just the girl with the dead dog and the dead mom. Sometimes, I have really bad days, I get really anxious and depressed. I am doing everything in my power to get better. I went to rehab every day for years. I don't drink. I sleep more than the proper amount.

People have been getting hit by cars for a long time, probably since cars were first introduced. Still, so much is unknown. The first pedestrian in the United States reported to be hit by a car, and unfortunately die, was Henry Bliss at age 69.[3] His accident happened on September 13, 1899. Over 100 years ago. Bliss was hit in New York City by an electric taxicab. He died the next day. On the internet, when you Google the first person ever to be hit by a car, all that comes up is death. I couldn't find records about people who were hit by cars and survived.

I am grateful to be alive. To have survived a horrible accident. To be coming out on the other side. I've spent entire years resenting the woman who hit me. That won't change anything. It's still just a thing that happened. This book documents my journey trying to claw my way out of the depths this fiasco has put me in.

---

3   Eschner, K. (n.d.). Henry Bliss, America's First Pedestrian Fatality, Was Hit By an Electric Taxi. *Smithsonian Magazine*. https://www.smithsonianmag.com/smart-news/henry-bliss-americas-first-pedestrian-fatality-was-hit-electric-taxi-180964852

it was destiny
when i was hit by a car
pretty messed up, huh?

chapter 2

learning how to walk and talk again

i am different
i'm getting better each day
changed forever

One of the first things I remember was being at Texhoma where I was transferred in early November 2019. That's almost two months of nothingness. I was alive, in a near coma, and new memories were not registering for a while after I came to.

Texhoma is a skilled nursing facility, a "SNF." It is a residence turned neurological rehab unit in Los Angeles. It was part of a group called CareMeridian, later named Neuro Restorative. It was called Texhoma in conversation because it was on Texhoma Street.

There were nurses there round the clock, assistant nurses, a cook, and the big three: a physical therapist (Kaitlyn), a speech therapist (Jackie), and an occupational therapist

(Mike). The team guided me through many firsts. It is where I first sat up, stood up, and began saying a few words.

Before Texhoma, I was just lying in different beds in different facilities where professionals cared for my unresponsive body and injured brain. I couldn't open my eyes for more than a few seconds. When they were open, they were unseeing. I have heard that I had the best, zit-free skin and had lost over twenty pounds. It wasn't worth it.

I had a room by myself, zipped up into a unique type of bed every night and any time when no one was in my room. It was called a Posey bed, and Diana had to sign a consent form for its use as it was considered a restraint. I kept flinging my body around and almost falling out when the Posey bed was open. I would say I was just stretching. So, they would zip it up when I was alone and every night before I went to sleep to keep me safe. They would open it when the nurses or my family and friends were in the room.

I couldn't talk when I first got to that house. I communicated by pointing at things on a sheet filled with pictures and labels. It was a huge deal the first time I showed an understanding of the correlation between pictures and words.

I would point at these tiny cartoons of a bed, a TV, or the toilet. Jackie helped me learn how to communicate again. At first, I just made sounds. I pointed on a whiteboard or did thumbs up and thumbs down for yes and no.

I would refuse to shower sometimes. The nurses would tell me to get up to wash my body. I would quietly whisper no or shake my head if I felt grumpy. When I started to talk again, I mumbled, because I couldn't control the muscles in my mouth, and I had zero lung capacity left. For many, many months, I could only whisper. I'm generally a very loud girl, so that was very unlike me.

At the beginning of Thanksgiving week, I was still only pointing at things. On Thanksgiving Day, I spoke my first word in two and a half months.

I whispered, "Bathroom."

My dad was with me, and my aunt had been on her way out but returned for something. Diana was so happy she didn't miss my first word. At that point, they were trying to train me out of the need to wear diapers. So, they started to try to have me tell them when I needed to go to the bathroom instead of just going. Success!

While staying at Texhoma, I had just started getting my bearings back, starting to realize what had happened to me. One day when I was with my dad, probably watching "The Office," I said straight-faced and very seriously, "I got fucked up bad."

It was all sinking in, and I was as angry as someone could be without their brain fully working. My whole body filled with rage. I felt pure hatred for that woman for a long time. I will always be very pissed off at her, but I can also see her as a person who just made a horrible mistake. One that I had to pay the price for, for some messed up reason.

One of my first full conversations was also with my dad.

"I want to go home," I whispered. And then I asked my dad if he had a car.

"I do," he answered.

"Let's go," I said, thinking he would help me escape.

"Where is home?" he asked.

"Diana's," I said.

They weren't sure whether I remembered that my mom had died and that I had been living at my aunt's when I wasn't at school. I knew enough to know I shouldn't be living in a hospital. The first thing I wrote when they gave me a whiteboard to start trying to write was that I wanted to leave. I didn't want to be there at all.

I don't think I knew why I was there at that point. I'm only assuming, but I probably thought an unnamed villain was forcing me into some kind of captivity.

Very early on, Diana asked me who she was, and she wrote two names on a whiteboard. I pointed to our friend Linda's name instead of hers! I laughed when I heard this story. I don't know for sure, but I think I was more confused by the pointing part of their question than by who they were.

As bad as my memory was, I have never forgotten a person. Even casual acquaintances. I know that it's all up there. It's just hiding from me. Like, I remember all the names of my elementary school teachers and the words to songs I'd listened to on repeat.

I knew which songs were my favorites and when they were my favorites. Then a few memories of college. I don't even remember graduating college or ever having sex with anyone. I remember the people I've been intimate with, but that's about it.

I talked to my therapist from Arcata over the phone once I moved back to LA. She started quizzing me on that period of my life. The five years I say I don't remember. And since she was my therapist for most of that time, she knows more than I do about that time. We did these quizzes irregularly, but I got every question she asked me right.

My first PT when I was conscious again was Kaitlyn. She helped me start sitting, standing, and walking. I first sat up at the beginning of my recovery two and a half months after the accident, and I would start to fall over instantly. I didn't have strength in my abs or any muscles in my core.

Once I was able to sit, then I could begin standing. I had to wear hi-tops Diana bought for me to support my ankles. After I started walking, I needed shoes in different sizes because I had to wear a splint and an AFO (ankle foot orthotic) on my right leg to support my ankle while walking.

Diana went out and bought some shoes for me to pick from. I picked a pair of orange shoes from her choices, but later I didn't like my choice at all. I ultimately donated the shoes and the splints when I had no use for them anymore, and they could help someone else. As much as I deeply despised them, I'll admit that they did help me.

As part of my occupational therapy, Mike helped me learn how to shower again and to dress. He also let me cook. The first time I baked cookies again was with him. Mike worked closely with Kaitlyn. He was the one who brought someone in to help measure the limbs on my right side to make the AFO for my right ankle and knee.

A different group made splints for my right wrist and my right arm. Even though I didn't like them, I had to use them because they were helping me. I wore them for many months, but by March 2020, I at least stopped having to wear the AFO to walk. However, I had to continue with the ones that used tension to extend my arm and leg muscles.

For more information about some of the therapies, devices, and tools used throughout my recovery, please see the list of resources at the end of this book.

Two days before Christmas, I told Diana in a troubled tone that I didn't get any presents. She reassured me and told me not to worry. She said that we still had time before Christmas and that I had already received some presents for Hanukkah. I got very frustrated with her for responding to me in this way. I repeated it, now a little bit noticeably annoyed and angry. Diana didn't understand why this was happening. Why was I getting so worked up over this? So I repeated, "I didn't get any presents!"

Then I had enough time to think and rephrased it and said that I hadn't gotten *anyone else* gifts for Christmas. She then understood I wasn't talking about receiving presents but buying them for others.

After I had finally gotten my message across, Diana helped me make a list of what I could get people. That wasn't enough for me, though. I told her, almost through tears, that if I sent her out to buy gifts from me, I still wouldn't be the one buying them.

My aunt said that no one expected a gift from me that Christmas but nonetheless braved going to the mall the day before Christmas and bought the presents I asked her to get. She also brought cards so I could dictate a note and sign my name with my left hand.

The nurses at Texhoma were so lovely to me. I really liked one of them, Idalia, the most because she was funny and made me laugh. At that point, I could only receive what people were saying and couldn't express much as a response. I don't remember much about being there. My brain wasn't able to hold on to things that were happening.

But once I started talking, I always told them I wouldn't miss any of them and hated it there. I did miss them. I went back there once I was better, almost two years after being a patient. To show them whom I have become and tell them I was wrong when I said I wouldn't miss them.

When I started talking in mid-November, it was only in a whisper, and I would only speak to Jackie. I don't know whether I was too shy to use my voice or if I just hadn't found my post-accident voice yet. I wouldn't even talk to my family. Now, you can't shut me up.

However, I wasn't comfortable enough to speak casually when I was at Texhoma. It's sad for me to think about this time. First, I have no memory of it, and two, a quiet version of me is opposite from my current self. It's hard and weird to reconcile the two.

Briefly, people thought there was a chance I would die or be a vegetable forever. Thankfully, neither happened. Diana believed I would get better, but there was also a chance I would not. She was scared to be too optimistic because although she felt good about it, there was still a tiny chance that I would never live a completely normal life. What is normal, though? I will live the life I am supposed to.

My time here on earth is just going to be *different*. A close friend told me about her dream from when I was hit. She dreamed of me getting on a train and waving goodbye to her. She's very spiritual, so she took that to mean I was moving on to my next life. I waved goodbye to her and my current life. That didn't happen, though. I wouldn't write this book if I were dead or a vegetable.

I have absolutely no memory of the places I was at before the Texhoma nursing facility. No memories of Barlow Hospital. Or of the emergency room right after the accident; nothing from my time in the ICU, either. It's weird to know you were somewhere existing, but you have nothing to back it up.

My first new memories are from around two months after the accident, when I was stable enough to leave the acute care unit at Barlow and transfer to the nursing home. I guess that's when my brain could finally hold on to new memories. I finally reentered my body there. I existed very flatly during all that time. I couldn't speak in full sentences while I was there. At least I had started speaking at all.

It was where I took my first steps after being stuck in a hospital bed for so long. Someone had to hold on to a belt tied around my waist (called a gait belt) while I took those steps. It would be months of intensive rehab at another hospital and at CNS before I could walk alone without assistance. Independently.

For a few months, I could barely read a whole page. However, I never forgot how to read or how to spell. Now, I'm typing up page after page. I've read at least a chapter in a book every night. That's pretty unbelievable when you think of the fact that I was still minimally conscious less than a year before I first wrote this paragraph.

My body was still in trauma mode. I didn't get my period for about three and a half months. My body was in shock, forever recovering from a trauma. When I finally got my period, the Texhoma house didn't have the supplies to deal with it because they usually cared for older people.

For those three months, my period was the talk of the town. Diana and one of our family friends always asked the nurses if I had gotten it, like I was a 15-year-old who had never had a period before and was way past due.

In December 2019, an investigator from the court came to see me at Texhoma about appointing my aunt as my conservator. I was barely whispering at the time. He first asked me who Diana was. I said she was my aunt. He asked if she was my mom's or my dad's sister. I clarified that we weren't blood relatives. She had been my mom's best friend. Then he asked me if I was comfortable with her making medical and financial decisions. I nodded and whispered, "Yes."

It was only three months after a freaking motor vehicle had hit me, so I still wasn't super responsive. No one knew how much information had stuck in my brain. New things I remembered came out in this interview. The investigator asked me if I had a job. I looked at him like he was asking me what I thought to be an idiotic question. I answered no. He asked me if that meant I was a student. I said yes. He asked me where I went to school, and I said Humboldt State University. He asked me what I studied. I whispered back, "Environmental studies," the biggest word I'd said post-traumatic brain injury. He was asking me the most complicated questions anyone had asked me since my accident.

Last, he explained what a conservatorship was and that he needed to get my consent. He asked whether I understood what Diana was asking to be, what a conservator was. Conservatorship isn't the easiest concept to understand, and I had only recently woken up from my near-coma state. However, I nodded and whispered, "Yes," and he asked me to state what she was asking. Diana handed me a marker and the whiteboard that I had recently started using. In shaky letters I wrote, "make decis."

They knew I meant decisions and that I understood this complex concept! It was a big turning point. No one knew what I would say to him, but it was something we needed to do for the legal ramifications. I ended up saying what I was supposed to say. I honestly don't know what would have happened had I said anything else in response to his questions.

At Texhoma, I was obsessed with sleeping. I had convinced myself that I wasn't sleeping through the night. Traumatic brain injuries affect many things, like the ability to sleep or to visualize. For me, that means no dreaming. For so many others affected, it means only nightmares for some reason.

I prefer my dreamless nights over having only nightmares. I wasn't able to articulate that I wasn't dreaming, so my problem became that I wasn't sleeping. I got one of my doctors to prescribe me powerful sleeping medication.

The doctor prescribed Trazodone, an anti-depressant used as a sleep aid and for anxiety. I would start asking about it right after lunch to ensure they gave it to me at night. I would ask countless times. I don't know whether I didn't trust them or why I was so suspicious. I would complain and tell Diana to ensure they gave me them.

I told her I hadn't slept the night before and just laid awake for hours. She would assure me that, yes, I had slept. After a few days of this happening, she talked to some of the nurses in the house. She told me that multiple nurses saw me fast asleep numerous times throughout the night.

My feeding tube was taken out in December but my trach had to wait. They left scars I will maybe have forever. One smack dab in the middle of my neck and another indentation of a scar towards the left side of my tummy tattoo. In January 2020, the nurses had begun putting a cap on the hole in my neck for short periods. To see if I could breathe, swallow, and talk without it.

Later that month, the trach came out too. Taking it out was anticlimactic after waiting for so long. They just pulled it out of my neck. They let me see it after it was out—just a piece of unassuming-looking metal. I was finally free of all medical devices! I was thrilled all the tubes were out of my body.

I did not have any foreign objects in me anymore! I will have scars for a very long time. Maybe forever. During the pandemic we went through in Spring 2020, I did my rehab via Zoom and I could see my neck all the time. I started to focus on my trach scar, an angry-looking reddish circle in the middle of my neck.

I also had a soft pinkish little spot in my stomach where the feeding tube had been. My battle scars. For a while, I wanted to see a plastic surgeon about getting my trach scar covered up. They take skin from another part of your body and cover the scar in the middle of your throat with it.

Instead, in Fall 2020, when doctors' offices opened again, I saw a dermatologist who recommended a silicon scar removal cream for most of my scars since my chest tube and feeding tube scars had mostly healed. He zapped my trach arecells in your skin.

After each treatment, the scar got an ugly red, but after months of treatments, the color and texture of the scar improved significantly. Now, I just wear my favorite choker with a small mirror as a pendant that fits perfectly over the scar.

you know what they say
when it rains, it pours- I think
that's my life right now

chapter 3

getting ready to move back home

writing this book
makes me feel weirdly in touch with
myself through all this

After three months at Texhoma, in February 2020, I went to Northridge Hospital's acute rehab unit to prepare to go home. I was so much better when I left Texhoma that Diana could drive me to Northridge Hospital in her car, after learning how to assist me in getting in and out of a vehicle, of course. A few months before, I had to go by ambulance to Texhoma from Barlow, while I was still blissfully unaware. Just sleeping.

I didn't like being on Northridge's acute rehab floor. It was a hospital. More of a hospital than Texhoma had been—or even Barlow, although I have no memory of being at Barlow.

At Northridge, random nurses would wake me up often during the night, mostly to give me pills and medications, but sometimes for no reason. One time, they got me up just to pee. It was not because I had told them I had to pee but because they woke me up and basically told me to.

Other times, they took my temperature and gave me medication throughout the night. The point is that they woke me up often during the night, but I would just go back to sleep. I'm lucky that I can fall asleep quickly and easily.

I could eat and drink by the end of December 2020, meaning I could finally be off the feeding tube, even though it left a scar that isn't showing any signs of fading. I am a vegetarian, and all the hospitals I was in were aware of it. While fed through a feeding tube, they gave me vegetarian, organic liquid food Diana got for me on Amazon.

I don't really remember any of the nurses at Northridge. That speaks for itself. They weren't memorable. Sometimes in the hospital, the nurses took forever to come and take me to the bathroom. It would take them five or even ten minutes at worst, but it seemed like forever.

I didn't have control of the muscles in my bladder yet, so I had been wearing diapers up to that point. They were trying to transition me back into regular undies. They inadvertently forced me to hold my pee.

A few times, I couldn't hold it in. Maybe one or two times, I peed in my pants. The only time I distinctly remember it happening, Diana was collecting my clothes to do my laundry and asked me why my pants were so wet. I was embarrassed and told her I had been sweating a lot during the night.

I don't remember my doctor there off the top of my head, but I do remember when Diana would tell me about him and remind me about him. I liked him because he always kneeled, squatted, or leaned down to make eye contact when talking to me. Many doctors did that for me—probably more who did than those who didn't.

I do remember my speech therapist from that hospital. We went to Starbucks once, and she made me order for my-self and then told me to figure out the change.

She also gave me things to take home. I don't know what to call them, but I used them as breathing treatments. For one of them, I sucked a hard breath in, and there was a mea-suring thing that would move with my breath. You put some warm water in the other one and then blow bubbles.

There's also an option where you hummm into it, and say whoooooooo, and do highs and lows with your voice. It seemed silly then, but it helped strengthen my lungs and vocal cords.

I had two occupational therapists there. One gave me showers and she trained my family on what to do when I was home. The other one cooked with me and helped me to finish art projects. We made cookies and mac-and-cheese.

The kitchen and its use in therapy was one of the rea-sons that the Northridge rehab unit was chosen for my acute rehab stay. I love to cook, and my family knew I would like this. Performing functional tasks you enjoy is an important part of successful occupational therapy. My OT also had me write a poem with felt letters and decorate it for my girl-friend at the time. These sessions were a welcome change after lying in bed for so long.

My therapists there worked me harder than I had worked before at that point in my recovery. However, it was so neces-sary. The exercises hurt my hands, which weren't working at all. The PT got me a new walking splint (a new AFO) so that

I could walk with greater comfort. I didn't like the previous one because it was heavy and cumbersome. So, she got me a lighter one made of plastic instead of metal.

I practiced going up and down steps with the physical therapist so that I could walk into our home. There are steps to go into the house. They would say "up with the good, down with the bad" to remind me how to do steps without them. I will probably never forget this saying. By April 2020, I didn't even need the AFO anymore.

Last, but certainly not least, I got Botox shots into my right arm and hand muscles at Northridge in February 2020. They helped me tremendously. Before getting the injections, I couldn't open or stretch my hand. My right hand and arm hurt before I got the shots.

The shots loosened my muscles so much that my hand finally opened up and didn't hurt as much anymore. It was at that point that I started to use my right hand. Before, it was stiff, like uncooked spaghetti against my torso.

While my right arm and hand were rigid and contracted, my left hand was still very weak so I needed help eating all my meals while in the hospital. They would ask me what I wanted to eat first and next and next.

Sometimes though, they just dropped off food, and no one came to help me, so I just had to stare at the food. I would have to press a button and call for help. I didn't feel embarrassed to ask for help.

I am now also okay with anyone seeing me naked because so many people had done so during my hospitalization. I love sunbathing in the nude, or at least topless, and it became habitual on the empty and isolated beaches in the Pacific Northwest.

Free the nipple! All bodies are beautiful—normalize nudity. Being naked while others bathed and changed me felt natural.

I don't remember much about my time in the hospitals. There are considerable gaps in what I do remember. I don't think my brain was holding on to new memories then. For some reason, I remember the most random, obscure parts, one thing in particular.

While I was at Northridge, I had to wear this yellow bracelet that said, "FLIGHT RISK." I don't know why I remember that or even why specifically I remember the color. I even had yellow fabric ties around the ends of my bed. They were terrified that I would try to make my exit. The funny thing is I couldn't even walk alone at that point in my recovery. Someone always had to be next to me, and they would hold on to me so I wouldn't fall.

Most of my more concrete memories from those months of my life are attributed to my time at Northridge Hospital. I was in the Texhoma nursing home for the longest chunk of time but don't remember that much. Even though I was at Northridge for the shortest time compared to Barlow and Texhoma, it was just three weeks, it became the background of many memories. I always think I was in that hospital for any memory I held on to in my brain.

I was barefoot most of my time in these medical facilities. I didn't wear shoes for four months after my accident. Every time I had to pee, a nurse put these horrible, tan, nonstick socks on my feet. Without fail, they made sure I was wearing these socks.

I don't think people can fall barefooted, and I'm pretty sure our feet have something akin to nonslip on the bottom of them. I walk around at home barefoot. I couldn't do it there, though. They were probably just covering their bases and ensuring I didn't fall under their care and then sue them, but the socks stuck out.

I found out what day I would go home and leave Northridge Hospital. From then on, I was in countdown mode for a while. I was very excited not to be in a hospital. At that point, I had been in and out of medical facilities for five and a half months! So, I was extremely excited to leave them and just be at home. I remember, at first, it was six more days. Then five more days, four more days, and so forth, until it was finally my last day living in a hospital. I was beyond excited.

The day after I got home was also the day that Diana's father's ashes went into his resting place at the military cemetery. So many people came to the house for a small celebration of his life. My aunt's brother and sister-in-law came from Puerto Rico. My girlfriend at that time came to be with me. I was back in the real world.

here I am, injured
but slowly getting better
it takes a long time

chapter 4

healing our bodies, but not healing our planet

the world is changing
faster than we can cope with
so we are behind

I got a tiny water bottle with every meal at Northridge Hospital. It was SO STUPID. I would never ask for it. I probably haven't used a single-use plastic water bottle on purpose since middle school.

At the first hospital I was placed in, up in Eureka, I was told they threw away their yellow paper scrubs after going into my room only once. They used so many gloves, a ridiculous number of gloves. The medical facility system is probably the worst at sustainability. This was before COVID precautions when it became even worse.

When I was both cognitively ready and able to ask, I asked my aunt to bring me my reusable metal water bottle from home. Ultimately, I couldn't even use it because it was very heavy. It was too heavy to hold up to my mouth to drink when my hands and wrists were so weak and weren't working yet.

I asked Diana to bring me one of my water bottles that was made of plastic, much lighter than my 32-oz metal hydro flask. I remember it was a green one that said "Humboldt State" on it. Afterward, I got a little yellow hydro metal flask to take to rehab at the Centre for Neuro Skills (CNS), my next stop on the infinite journey to recovery.

My 32-ounce bottle was too heavy to bring to the clinic in my backpack, so I used this new smaller flask until I was discharged from CNS. My old yellow bottle holds much more water than the smaller one. Water is so important. Water is life.

There are many things in my life I have forgotten. Memories that just flew out of my head. I can't picture being in class during my almost five-year-long stay in Humboldt County enrolled in college, but I do mostly remember what I learned as an environmental studies major. Not facts or figures, but the big picture stuck with me.

I also remember things I did to reduce waste. In all the houses I lived in, we had a compost bucket to empty into a compost pile or into a green bin when there was no compost pile. In the last and best house where I lived in Arcata, we had a compost pile in our garden and a contraption that would turn it into usable compost. That house was affectionately called the Ruff House after the two dogs who lived there. I later implemented a compost bucket in my aunt's house and then in my apartment to be emptied into the green garbage bin.

At Northridge Hospital, they sent me a small carton of milk with every meal. I don't even drink cow's milk. So my dad called the food service people soon after I voiced my discontent with the milk cartons. He told them to send me plant-based alternatives if they had to send milk.

Then, they at least started to send almond milk, but only after a second call to stop sending me cow's milk! They shouldn't have kept doing something after I asked them not to, and someone should have realized that I sent it back every day to get thrown away.

They also sent a banana with every meal. Diana would take them home because I didn't eat just plain bananas unless they were covered in peanut butter or blended into a smoothie. I had no blenders readily available at that point. Food services kept sending them even though they would usually come back to them uneaten.

We never told them to stop. Even though we probably should have. Everything unused probably got thrown away, including all those bananas. That made me feel sad because someone could have used it all.

To add insult to injury, the hospital staff brought me a packet of hot sauce with every breakfast I ate. With eggs, it made sense, and I always used it, but it didn't make any sense when it came with my pancakes or a bowl of cereal. They brought me a hot sauce, no matter what I had ordered for breakfast.

Once, I asked them why they were bringing me hot sauce even when I was eating something that would be ridiculous to put hot sauce on. They responded that they were just doing what they were told to do. What a waste!

There is a concept known as "zero waste" that I try to practice. It is basically not creating any waste at all. It's hard. I did that primarily by using reusable water bottles. Even though plastic water bottles are just a fraction of the waste that humans make.

When I shopped in college, I always brought and continued to bring reusable bags. I always tried to buy as much as I could without packaging. I made a face and body scrub out of coffee grounds. According to the United Nations, if food waste were represented as a country, it would be the third largest producer of greenhouse gases, and we could feed about two billion people globally with the food that goes uneaten.

How do we reach zero waste? The Environmental Protection Agency breaks down the reduction of food waste into different categories.[4] A few apply here.

First is prevention, which is stopping waste from even occurring by using and serving just what is needed. Like at the hospital, they shouldn't give patients food and drinks they do not want or ask for and continuously do not eat and send back!

Next is recovery, which describes the donation and redistribution of food to other people. So, hospitals shouldn't just throw away the food that isn't eaten but instead give it to people who need it.

Last is recycling, the process of changing waste into other products. Hospitals could do any of these three things instead of throwing away everything.

I was in the hospital system for over five months, aware and conscious for at least half that time. The amount of good, usable stuff I saw thrown into the trash was ridiculous. I can't even put it into words.

---

4   EPA. (2023, October). *Wasted Food Scale*. www.epa.gov/sustainable-management-of-food.

They just threw away thing after thing, and that was just what I saw. I'm sure what goes on where there are no witnesses is worse. I think every hospital should have a sustainability coordinator to make sure what they're doing is responsible. Honestly, though, that's probably wishful thinking.

According to a quick Google search, there are over 300 hospitals in California alone.[5] As of October 2023, there were over 6,000 hospitals in the United States, according to the American Hospital Association.[6] I'm sure they're each as bad as the next one when it comes to dealing with and disposing of waste.

It's scary and even more alarming to consider the whole world. Waste is the least of their concerns, especially in developing countries lucky enough to have hospital access. Then it becomes anxiety-inducing when you also think about all the hospitals, schools, and restaurants in the world. All the uneaten food just gets put in the garbage while there are so many hungry bellies.

During my junior, senior, and super senior years at Humboldt State, I was the education coordinator for WRRAP (Waste Reduction and Resource Awareness Program). In that role, I helped to plan and host a zero waste conference, an opportunity for people in the community to talk to students about what their businesses were doing regarding environmental efforts.

We had community and university speakers discussing things like the Arcata Recycling Program. We even had someone from the Environmental Protection Agency talk. I

5   Statista. (2023, November 30). *Number of hospitals in U.S. by state 2022*. https://www.statista.com/statistics/710528/hospital-number-in-us-by-state/
6   *American Hospital Association homepage | Hospitals USA | AHA*. (2024, February 1). American Hospital Association. https://www.aha.org/

was proud to bring the concept of food waste into the minds of so many students.

I tried to get the powers at CNS to put a recycling bin in the PT gym. They only offered plastic cups when someone wanted water and didn't bring a water bottle. Those cups got thrown into the garbage. One of my physical therapists said I should make that into my final capstone project on my way out of CNS.

A final rehab capstone project didn't exist there, but it was nice to leave it slightly more environmentally friendly than it had been during my time there, since they helped me so much. I try to leave the places I go to a little better than how I found them, whether that means picking up trash or fully putting out and cleaning up after a beach bonfire!

They changed directors near the end of my time at CNS, so when Victoria's office door read Director of Rehab, I confidently brought my ideas to her and she loved the concepts. They had a recycling bin already in the patient lunchroom and one in the staff lunchroom. I suggested at least moving one into the gym. I eventually convinced Victoria to order three more recycling bins for the clinic.

We placed one in the physical therapy gym, one in the occupational therapy wing, and the last in their lobby. It took me more than a year to get the recycling bins, and it only happened because I walked into the boss lady's office and practically ordered them myself. I tried to introduce composting, but she was not interested at that time.

Don't even get me started on how bad the coronavirus has been for the environment. Countless plastic gloves straight into the trash. Infinite paper masks. So many plastic and paper take-out containers that the country almost ran out of ketchup packets! Companies and organizations worked tirelessly to make the pandemic easier on our poor planet. Hospitals need to do their part too! Households around the world are struggling with how to handle our waste. When it comes to a hospital scale or in schools across the globe, we're at a loss for dealing with not just food waste but all waste.

Avoiding food waste also offers a solution to the problem of hungry people. According to the organization Rescuing Leftover Cuisine, one out of eight people experiences food insecurity, and 40% of the food in this country gets wasted.[7]

We produce more than enough food to feed everyone, so why are there hungry people? Food gets distributed and thrown away in ways that leave empty, hungry bellies. Hospitals are just one example out of countless others that do not handle food or waste properly. Hospitals may be healing us, but they are ignoring our planet.

sometimes i wonder
what is the point of our lives–
who makes the choices?

---

7   Cuisine, R. L. (n.d.). *Rescuing leftover cuisine.* https://www.rescuingleftovercuisine.org/

chapter 5

my loved ones, old and new

i miss my dog, ted
he once traded in his life
here i am, alive

I am very thankful for everyone who helped me and continues to help me. The first couple days after the accident, my Humboldt friends, my dad, my aunt, Kyle, and his girlfriend (who later became his wife) were by my side. My dad stayed with me the whole time and when Diana had to leave, my late mom's husband came to help my dad at the hospital in Eureka.

What really helped was when my cousin, Ike, called my aunt and connected her with his brother-in-law, a trauma doctor. He knew what needed to happen, in what order, and what to ask.

During those first two weeks, he talked to Diana a lot to guide her through the medical decisions and to ensure I went to the right places. My aunt and her friends in Los Angeles did a lot of research about places for me to go for treatment and to locate neurologists in Los Angeles. One of them put us in contact with a neurologist at UCLA who subsequently saw all my brain scans and guided Diana in my treatment.

Many of my mom's friends visited me at Barlow Hospital in Los Angeles when I hadn't even woken up yet. I was never alone. Even unconscious. Everyone was somber as they wished I could respond to them. Diana sang to me and played music. My mom's book club friends read books to me. One of them sang to me, too.

Our friend, Linda, was consistently by my side in and out of hospitals. She talked to my doctors, went with Diana to different facilities to help her choose the best one because two sets of eyes are better than one. She helps drive me around. Many of my therapists knew her because she used to pick me up from CNS, and to this day, we get together almost weekly with our dogs for coffee or boba.

Kyle started attending a support group for friends and family of people who have suffered brain injuries. He started about a month after I was hurt and went for about three months before it stopped because of the coronavirus. The events of September 7th impacted everyone who loved me. They weren't physically injured, but they were hurt emotionally. We were all injured by that woman's mistake. She might have killed Teddy and hit only me with her car, but so many people were also profoundly affected.

Some middle and high school friends of mine came to see me at Barlow and every medical facility that followed. People came from near and far to visit me. They came down from Arcata, all over the San Fernando Valley, and my grandfather and his wife even came from Pennsylvania.

I had a network of people that came to support me. People that were friends of my mom's, my friends going as far back as elementary school, and all my roommates and friends throughout college.

Some of those people left me gifts and tokens to show support beyond their visits. We know who gave me most of the gifts, but there was one thing, a purple orchid specifically, that has never been traced back to anyone. I even had Diana send an email to everyone that came regularly to see me asking who brought the flower. No one claimed to have brought the flower. It remains a mystery.

Unfortunately, the flower died before I even came home from the hospital. I've been told orchids are really hard to keep alive, so I'm not taking the blame!

My dad compiled a list of people to cover shifts, which was fine while I was minimally and barely conscious. Every weekend, my dad would make a schedule for the following week. He would email the 17-or-so people who had volunteered to come and spend their time with barely-conscious me, except for late at night when I was asleep.

Someone was always with me, especially when I was at Barlow and was still basically in a coma. At that point, I couldn't advocate for myself yet. They were also there to stimulate my mind constantly while I was unresponsive.

However, months later, when I was at Texhoma, the people in charge told my family nicely that I needed some rest time. Alone. So they started scheduling empty shifts on purpose, to give me some quiet time.

Getting everyone to cover their shifts during the holidays was hard. Diana desperately texted everyone she could think of, and my friends from all over the place answered her call.

A friend from middle school and friends from college came to cover an hour.

People came from as far away as Orange County and San Diego to cover a shift with me. They called themselves Team Emily. My dad says they were more like Emily's Angels. I feel so loved and so lucky to have had Team Emily.

I am incredibly thankful every day to be doing as well as I am. I would like to take all the credit, and my hard work is responsible for most of my healing, but it wouldn't have been possible without Team Emily, my loved ones and every therapist, doctor, and nurse who worked with me.

I still can't walk one hundred percent—my gait is off, and I do lose my balance sometimes. I can't use my right arm to do everything I want it to do, or dream at night, or remember all the significant events that have happened in my life. Every day became a struggle for me, but I have come face to face with the darkest parts of what could have happened.

Kyle came to visit me in November 2020 when I was barely sitting up alone and could just point to things I wanted. When he saw me months later, I was walking independently and talking up a storm. He cried when he saw me. A lot had changed since he had seen me at the hospital up in Eureka, and although he'd been getting updates from Diana, the difference between me in late 2020 and me at Texhoma was like night and day. A little more than a year had passed.

Several close friends and my then-girlfriend packed all my stuff from up north and drove them down to SoCal. They then unpacked it all. I have always had a ton of little things. Seemingly infinite little knick-knacks. They wanted to bring home everything for me. I didn't get to choose yes or no for anything. I didn't see most of the stuff they brought down until months later.

They did a great job with what they chose to bring down for me. I have most of my things, even small tchotchkes from various trips I went on and all my beanies and bags. The two things I am missing, though, and no one seems to know where they are, are all my belts and velvet scrunchies. Maybe they're together somewhere in the world. Not being worn or used. I have no idea where they could be.

Most of what I wore at the beginning when I had just started wearing clothes again was as stretchy as possible. My right arm was very rigid at that point. They had finally told my aunt to send me some clothes when I was at Texhoma and still in diapers but wearing some real clothes. Not my clothes yet, but anything was better than what they give you at a hospital.

Before that, for about two months, I wore only hospital gowns. When my legs went uncontrollably crazy, I kept exposing myself in the gown. So, they put me into stretchy hospital pants.

I've always considered wearing cute clothes as a way of making a statement to the world. I prioritize comfort and ease, so my style hovers somewhere between a homeless person, Adam Sandler, and an Urban Outfitters mannequin. I obsess over my clothes now because I went so long not getting to make any choices.

When I was still minimally conscious in the hospital, Julie, one of my best friends, would call and talk to me for twenty minutes or half an hour or more while Diana held up my phone for me to hear her voice. She lived in another state, so she couldn't visit me as quickly or as easily as she wanted to.

Julie would call me to talk. She wouldn't get any responses and would have a completely one-sided conversation.

She would gossip about people we went to high school with and tell me about her days. It was good for me to hear familiar voices at that point. Later in my recovery, when I was more aware, Julie did come to see me at the hospital or my house when I was home. We would sit together, chit-chat, or walk around my neighborhood.

The people that should be in my life are in my life and are talking to me regularly. The people who were vaguely close to me: classmates, distant friends, some coworkers from the years I was a camp counselor, and people I would just say, "Hi," to when I saw them aren't in my life anymore.

There are many people that I thought I was close to, but they haven't said a word to me after my accident. All it takes is a horrific, life-altering event to really show who should really be in your life.

Sometimes I wonder what I would do as an outsider in this situation. Would I be afraid to say something to someone who got hit by a car? If this had never happened to me, how empathetic would I be? How would I react if I had never been in this situation? I haven't been able to separate myself enough to feel okay that some people haven't and probably never will reach out to me about everything that has happened.

I was injured in a small town where everyone knew everyone. Maybe they were scared or didn't know what to say, so they've said zero words. No support or condolences for losing Teddy. I guess I thought we were closer than we were. As the years passed, they might have felt it had been too long to reach out.

I'm not going to call them out by name in case they read this book, but if they do read this book or to anyone reading this book, if someone you know gets in a horrific accident, always say something! It's better to say something and have it be wrong than to say nothing at all.

If I had died that day, I would've become everyone's best friend, regardless of whether we were friends or even knew each other. I know the people who didn't send me condolences, the people who didn't give me any acknowledgment that I was hit by a car, in some cases just miles away from where they lived, would have really made it seem like they were *so affected* by my theoretical death.

I am a social person. Super talkative. Very confident in my ability to be a friend.

An easy friend to make, but I felt like I was alone while working on my rehab at CNS because of the pandemic. Isolated. Only my dad and my girlfriend visited. Diana couldn't let many visitors come to our house because her elderly mother lives with Diana, and we had to be careful with her health.

At the clinic, no friends, only acquaintances. Except for my therapists. They became my closest friends for a while because this was mainly during the significant part of the pandemic, and no one was socializing. Before that, I was in a hospital surrounded by older people for six freaking months—no one around to be friends with me.

But then I met Hena in July 2020, who was doing rehab at CNS for one too many concussions. I don't remember how we met or started talking, but we became fast friends. A few months passed, and then we went to a nearby park and had McFlurries from McDonald's together. Hena could drive, and my aunt drove me to meet her. Hena ordered a fancy new flavor they were promoting and was subsequently disappointed. It was hot where we were, but we sat in the shade.

It was so nice talking to someone who *got* what I was going through. She knew the people I was talking about and agreed about those who annoyed me. That was probably one of the best parts I could say about someone who got on my nerves, and she knew exactly what I meant. Not only that, but Hena agreed about the people that bugged me.

I was going to rehab for three hours every day at that point. They knew we were friends, so we were scheduled as pairs all day. I laughed and hung out with my friend while I was going to therapy. It was the best of both worlds.

With Hena, we had this massive thing in common. Brain injuries. One of my therapists said it's the smart ones that make friends. So that this wouldn't be something we had to go through entirely alone. I still have a lot of love for my other friends and our relationships are still the same as be-fore my accident, even though many of them had seen me much worse off, just lying in a bed.

But none of them *get it*. They try to empathize and try hard to feel what I'm feeling, but I really hope they never truly understand it.

My closest friends saw me when I was still minimally conscious. There is still this huge thing that will always be different about our relationships now. It's not their fault, and I hope it never changes, but I have a brain injury, and they don't.

Even though I know it is the wrong way to think, I find myself feeling a little resentful of all the billions of people who have not had a brain injury. I know that is not the right way to think, and they're not thinking any less of me because I have a brain injury. I can't help it though.

That's why it's so nice to have friends who also have brain injuries. We have something in common, something I hope to never have in common with any of my other friends. It was nice to know I was not alone in this. I knew I wasn't dealing with any of this alone, and many people loved me dearly, but it was not the same. There is something hugely different between me and everyone I know. Something that will never change.

Hena was discharged in early April 2021. She was no longer there to joke around with or talk smack about certain therapists. There was really no one close to my age and ability level. No one to be friends with. I wasn't hoping for a cool 20-something-year-old to get a traumatic brain injury and be sent to CNS; I just got lonely there.

I became friendly with 30-, 40-, and 50-year-old patients there, but I would never hang out with them outside of CNS. With Hena leaving the clinic, my main in-clinic support system disappeared.

The types of people who were my friends at CNS were funny. Some middle-aged women and older men, people I'd never have become friends with under any other circumstance. My best CNS friend had been Hena, who was closer to my age, but when she was discharged, it then became this 40-something-year-old named Derek. He's a surfer dude. He had a skateboarding accident that put him in the hospital, and the doctors discovered he'd had a stroke.

We had been at CNS around the same time, and some days we were paired up for two hours. I liked him and think that in another life, we would be weed-smoking buddies. He dreamt of reentering the surfing world, and I supported him wholeheartedly.

At first glance, we didn't have anything in common. We were very different ages, and he used to be a surfer dude. We're both jokesters, we both have deficits, and we both chill extra hard. He is so optimistic and helped to motivate me. He was always cheering me on and loudly rooting for me. We were support systems for each other and stayed in each other's lives hanging out sometimes once we were both finished and discharged from CNS.

Towards the end of my time at CNS, I made two more friends who I am still friends with. Both are young; both had strokes at a young age.

Leili was paired with me a few times during PT. She has a dynamic personality and is very easy to talk to. We clicked. And Matt, he is another positive person like Derek. Always upbeat and cheering others on.

After leaving CNS, we continued to be in close contact and get together socially. We have brain injury play dates where we hang out with Hena and other rehab folks.

I was very vocal about my disappointment with my lack of friends at CNS. They can't magically make another girl my age appear, but my case manager and rehab director were trying. A young person's group for younger people with brain injuries was started at the clinic. My insurance didn't cover counseling groups for a while, so I had to pay for it on my own. I quickly decided that the group was not worth the money or my time.

It's hard for me when
I think about my past life
everything has changed

chapter 6

memories and dreams

I don't dream at night
I have not since I was hurt
will I dream again?

I don't remember lots of things from Emily 1.0's past.

I don't remember my college graduation in May 2019—just four months before the crash. I don't remember getting together with my former girlfriend. I don't remember going to Italy and then to Paris after my mom died or breaking my ankle after that trip.

I don't remember going to Hawaii multiple times to visit a best friend. I don't remember getting my nipples pierced. I don't remember ever walking any of the dogs I've had in my life. I don't remember when my mom was in the hospital. I don't remember the day of her death, after her quick winter decline and demise.

Such an odd assortment of things stayed in my brain. I remembered my mom was dead and that I lived with my aunt and not my dad when I would return to the Valley whenever I came home. I remembered the type of food Teddy ate and my Social Security number. I remembered we had lost my mom in 2017. I've never forgotten anyone's face, and I remembered most names.

Even the most random people from my college classes whom I never spoke to or hung out with outside of class. I remember all the important people like Diana, my dad, my brother and his wife, my grandma, mom's second husband, all of my cousins and my uncle. I remember all of my friends from that college town and all of my friends from elementary, middle, and high school.

I remember the addresses of everywhere I have lived. All my childhood homes. Each one of the three houses I lived in throughout college. I even remember the address we had to get our mail sent to in the dorms. I said them or wrote them down enough to have them stuck in my head.

I also remember the address of the house where I supposedly lived in New York on my fake ID, which I had from when I was 17 to 21: *167 Court St. Brooklyn, NY.* I also remembered my school ID number from Humboldt State. *2010978.* Even my driver's license number.

I guess there's something to be said about repeating something enough times and having it stick in your head. My brain got knocked around, and that information still stayed in my brain when many other things flew away.

I don't remember attending class in college either, but I always remembered that I had been studying environmental studies. I got my diploma despite having two classes to complete before the accident. I had enough credits to graduate, so my advisor at Humboldt State helped me and substituted classes for the remaining two requirements and determined that I didn't have to take them.

I thankfully don't remember getting hit or where I was walking when it happened. I don't remember where I was when I was in my near coma. I am beyond happy that I have no memory of this time. Even just hearing about it is scary. I know none of it was my choice or fault, but it still makes me feel sorry that I put everyone who loves me through all this.

In rehab, I also did cognitive rehab for 17 months to improve my memory. I mostly worked on my new short-term memory. I had to memorize numbers, I was told stories, and then I had to answer questions. I had to listen to and follow directions. Sometimes, I had to do memory tasks that are exactly what they sound like, where I had to remember to tell my cognitive therapist something after a few hours, then a few days. The last level of the memory tasks was remembering to do or say something two weeks later.

I ask people about the things I don't remember, but sometimes, I have spontaneous memories that just pop into my brain. I don't know what triggers them, and they seem so random. I found a second laptop in my room. At first, I was really confused. Why would I have two when the first one still worked?

Diana told me to try and charge it because it seemed out of juice. While it was charging, I suddenly remembered what had happened to it. I told my aunt that it wasn't just out of battery. It was *dead, dead*.

I had remembered that Teddy had spilled water on it the year before. I had been doing homework in my room, and there was a bowl of water in there for if he ever was thirsty when we were closed in my room at night. He ended up nudging the bowl and spilling it all over my laptop, breaking it instantly.

I'm no doctor, but I've watched enough medical TV shows and been around enough doctors to diagnose myself with retrograde amnesia due to an injury probably in my cerebellum. I haven't been able to dream since my accident. I had one dream, but I do not count it. People are telling me I am having dreams, just not remembering them.

I talked to my neurologist and asked her what to do about it. She told me I would eventually have dreams again, and probably already was, which was not helpful, and not happening. I just see the insides of my eyelids for the 8-10 hours I sleep each night.

I do hope I just need more time and to be even more patient because I hope to eventually have them again. I think maybe what people have been telling me is probably right: I am dreaming, but I'm just not remembering my dreams.

My eye doctor also suggested that possibly the problem is that I'm not entering REM when I sleep and, as a result, am not dreaming. He asked me if I would wake up feeling rested. I pretty much do, so I don't think that's it. I am hopeful that, eventually, the visual dreams will come back. However, I am simultaneously scared that the impact of the car might have taken that one thing away from me forever.

I have been told that I move around and make noises in my sleep. When dogs move their paws while they sleep or make noises, you know they are dreaming. My injury destroyed my ability to visualize many things; dreaming is all visualization. So again, maybe no dreaming for me.

In late September 2020, about a year after I was injured, I started having these feelings while I slept. There are no visualizations yet, so I can't call them dreams exactly—more like random and specific thoughts. I don't know these things but think they're a good sign. I think I might be dreaming, just without any accompanying visualization.

I also started having these dream-ish things in late January of 2021. I wouldn't visualize anything, but I would know what happened. Once, I had one where Teddy came to Humboldt my freshman year and another one where I was the one to break up with my most recent girlfriend. I don't know how it came into my brain because I saw nothing accompanying the feelings.

In the future, maybe I'll be able to see something. Now, I have also seen a color (blue)—a step in the right direction. I never remember seeing anything while sleeping, but I could remember whole dream stories, dreams I had before the accident. In one, I was camping in my car with Teddy on my college's campus. We went to get snacks from this food place they had on campus. Something he would never have been allowed to do, but it was in the dream realm, so it was allowed. Pretty elaborate, huh?

In early July of 2022, I was talking to one of my closest buddies from college. I asked her about my dreamlessness, and she gave me a response I'd never considered.

Maybe my body and brain are so tired that they genuinely need the time I'm sleeping to be purely for resting. I don't have the energy or capacity to spend my nights having mind-blowing realizations because my waking life is so full of metaphors.

My sleep time is for me to sleep, not have extensive, meaningful journeys. Or maybe it's just as simple as sleeping so soundly that I don't remember my dreams. Or I'm living a life in another dimension, and this is all the most detailed, the most screwed up, and the most life-like dream. Maybe this life is just a dream?

sometimes when i hear
about myself in the past—
doesn't feel like me

chapter 7

teddy, who would have died for me, and did

i think of teddy
a whole lot every day
that's what he deserves

"Where's Teddy?"
I asked my dad in December 2019, three months after the incident. I had only been speaking for a few weeks, and everyone was waiting and expecting me to ask.

It took my brain around three months to heal enough to ask where my partner in crime was. Luckily, I asked my dad. He had always watched Teddy when I was going somewhere dogs weren't allowed. My dad explained that I had been in a car accident, which I knew. He then told me that I had been walking with Teddy at the time of my accident.

This was new information to me. Even though it did not necessarily surprise me, he hadn't been smuggled in to see me at any medical facility I'd been in. I had known deep down that he was gone. I started crying so much that I was hyperventilating. I couldn't be comforted.

Everything he said was the wrong thing. I was stricken with grief. Everyone who knew about the accident already knew this, except for me. Everyone who loved me waited to tell me what had happened until I asked. When I was cognitively ready to ask that question, would I be ready for the answer?

I still don't feel ready. I don't think anyone ever would be. All day at CNS, I see people much worse off than me. That's Teddy's doing. I feel it in my bones, that his death was why my injuries weren't as bad as they could have been. To make sense of his death. Thinking that makes me feel better, to think I lived because he died, to think that his little body took the impact of the car before my body did. He was just a little guy, and I know he probably was walking in front of me, anyway, instead of next to me. I believe he somehow saved me, maybe more in a spiritual sense than a literal one.

I need his death to have meaning. So I continue to say he took the initial impact. Which he probably did. One of the reasons I went to counseling at CNS was because I was so stricken with grief. It was affecting my motivation to do my rehab exercises. My physical therapist told the counselor that I needed help, emotionally. The first few times I went and saw the counselor, I just cried because I hadn't gotten to the point of talking about him yet.

We were only supposed to go on a quick pee run. After more than two hours passed, one of my roommates, Alicia, walked down our street to see if I was close. She ran into some people who told her that a car had hit a dog. Her first thought was just about how devastated I would be. For a few minutes, she thought that only Teddy had been hit by the car and killed.

What I think is that my mom was with me when the car hit me, she was beside me, in Teddy maybe, to ensure I would live. I sometimes think she knew, and that's why she gave Teddy to me. I wasn't supposed to die on that day.

I imagine her as a tiny fairy flitting beside me that day. Maybe every day. She had to do work that day. Some hardcore magic. It saddens me to think she couldn't protect our innocent doggy. At least it was instant, quick and painless. The hardest thing about having one of the best dogs is that they don't live that long compared to us.

It's just extra hard to stomach that his death was so unnatural. Maybe if he'd stayed alive much longer, he would've had some terrible, painful disease. Or he could've had something happen that wasn't instantaneous. At least he didn't suffer. At least he didn't know what was happening. Everything just went dark.

Maybe I vaguely remember slowly waking up at Barlow Hospital. Bright lights, constant beeping. That all-too-familiar hospital smell. I was confused. Scared. My reaction was fitting for what happened. Probably a bit calmer than I should have been because my brain was just swimming. Nothing really sticking.

Months went by, and then one day, memories and higher levels of thinking were coming back. Then, more details came out. Teddy had taken the car's impact and died on the spot. I was beyond depressed at the news of what happened to my little dog. I'm still processing by writing many poems and reflecting. An elegy, to come to terms with it. I guess it was destiny that he died saving my life.

He gave his life for mine; my ferocious protector in a cute, 22-pound body. I am forever grateful to him. He probably saved my life. I will never forget him. Or even love another dog in the same way. He should have lived a full, long life.

I think that I truly woke up, snapping out of my time existing but not really being there, when I asked where Teddy was. My memories of him were deep in my head. Deep enough that it took me almost three months to question why the dog who had been by my side for over two years was no longer there. My mom had adopted him over three years before his untimely death. On her deathbed, she entrusted him to me. He was one of my last connections to her.

Based on what I've heard, we had been walking to the town's marsh. That was probably my favorite walk. It was so pretty and went past all the important parts of town. Lots of good, cool graffiti to look at on the way. The museum, the town square, the packing district. I don't know why I chose that street, at that time on that day. Or why the driver did.

Sometimes I think about those decisions. Why did I walk down the same street she was driving on? At least one beer in her stomach. Her choice changed both of our lives. Possibly forever. I will have a brain injury for the rest of my life. She'll have to go to sleep every night with the image of striking me with her car and killing an innocent, cute, little dog

One of my old roommates told me a story, one that I thought was very interesting. She told me that the week before our accident, Teddy was misbehaving. He bit our mailman and got into two dog fights, one with the dog we lived with and the other with a dog at the beach. It was a little bizarre, but he was feisty, and I had said there would be an earthquake or something. There really was an "or something."

We were hit by a car when we were just walking, like we had done every day, multiple times a day, for years. I think he knew on some level that it was going to happen. He was my protector, and he knew that his time as my guardian was ending, making me very sad. I loved him with all my heart. The driver took him away from me. And I will forever be so mad at her for doing that.

Teddy was an adorable dog. Maybe the cutest. He was pure goodness. He would snuggle up to go to sleep in a tent or the car, and would hike with me for miles. He was wise beyond his years. He always ate people's food even though he shouldn't have. Sourdough bread and french fries were his favorites. He could always sense me coming home and would start barking. He would sit in my room for hours and wait until I got home.

We hiked everywhere in Humboldt. Camped up and down the coast of California. He especially loved running free in open spaces. In Arcata, you were ten minutes from the river, the beach, or the marsh. I'd decide which place we'd go to each day. We could've been in three completely different environments.

He'd ride shotgun or even more reckless, on my lap looking out my window. He slept in my bed. He came with me to class. The teachers just dealt with it. Even if they didn't want him there, I would bring him anyway. I had a letter designating him as an emotional support animal so he was allowed to accompany me to class, out to dinner, and on planes.

I thought it was Teddy's birthday the day before our accident, so I threw him a party with his favorite people and he got lots of treats and cookies from everyone invited. It is comforting for me to think that I would have died the day I was injured had he not been literally by my side. He died for me.

Before he became my dog, Teddy wasn't so good. He used to bite, and my mom was even a little apprehensive around him when he was hers. Then when he became mine, I gave him all my love until he became a cuddle baby. I think it was all the attention he got as my dog.

I was at first a little hesitant to have a dog while in college. I remember not knowing how it was going to work. I ended up just bringing him to all my classes because at that point, he was a very good boy. He would just sit quietly under my desk until it was time to go.

I don't know Teddy's life before he found our family. I know he was at a shelter, though I don't know how long he was there, or how many shelters he'd been in before my mom adopted him. I do know he was a year-and-a-half when he became her dog. Then, he was almost three when he became my dog, and he was over five when he passed away.

There's a lot about his life I don't know about, but I do know that for years, he was my dog, and the year he was my family dog, he lived a great life. He went on planes, to class, and camping with me.

Teddy was a weird combination of my little brother and my son. My little brother because he was my mom's dog first and my son because I took him to the vet. He was my son when he was eating something he shouldn't be—my little brother when we played, went hiking, and went around town together. Sometimes, I was mom to him. Other times, I was the cool older sister. I always loved him. He was my partner in crime. One year, we were both hot dogs for Halloween; another, I was a lion tamer and he was my lion.

Then, he was killed by the reckless act of someone who never knew him. What she did is unforgivable. Maybe I'll come to a place of just disgust instead of hatred in the future. However, I will never forgive her. Forgiveness is good for your soul, but some actions are unforgivable. Not only did she leave me with irreparable emotional, physical, and cognitive deficits that I might forever need to work through, but she also killed my very best friend, my constant companion, the living reminder of my mom.

That woman's actions led to him losing his life while still fairly young. I can never, for his sake, forgive or forget what happened. At the crime scene, someone, and I don't know who, gave Teddy CPR. I am very grateful to that person.

They didn't want Teddy to die, so they tried as hard as they could to keep his little heart beating. I don't know how to find out who they are, but if they read this book, I want them to know how much I appreciate what they did.

In late 2020, I got a fish so I could care for and love another living being. He has since passed away because fish bought from a big tank at the pet store tend to not live very long. When I was at Petco getting him, I saw a cute dog that kind of looked like Teddy, at least they were both small and white. I instantly thought that was a sign from whomever that a fish wasn't my final pet.

Teddy was still watching over me. Linda said maybe it was a sign from Teddy that he was happy I would have a companion for a little bit until I was both physically and mentally ready to have a dog again.

My general plan for a long time was to get another dog on the third anniversary of my accident. I thought Teddy would metaphysically be closest to me on that day. I planned on going to the dog shelter to find them. I planned to have the dog choose me. I was also leaning towards getting a girl dog because Teddy was my last boy dog for a while.

I was thinking of naming them Pretzel because I thought of it and then heard it on a show and it is the freaking cutest dog name I've ever heard, unless they already have a cute name. I went on Petfinder occasionally after I got back from spreading Teddy's ashes in Arcata in February 2022. I was just browsing, seeing if any dog caught my eye. A few did, but they weren't easily accessible or were young puppies.

The first dog whose foster mom I talked to was a dog named Trey. Trey was the spitting image of Teddy—also a Lhasa apso and poodle mix. Only a year-and-a-half old, and he was living just a town over from me. He only had three legs because he was also hit by a car. It seemed like fate. He could be my chance to make it even with the universe for Teddy's death.

Adopting this injured little dog might have been my way of paying it forward. Taking care of him post-car accident like I never got to take care of Teddy. I emailed back and forth with the head of his rescue, and she put me in contact with Trey's foster mom.

We played phone tag for a while before finally connecting one Monday night. She told me he was potty trained but would wake up every morning at five or six to pee. I realized this was not the dog for me. Teddy would sleep from 11 at night to 11 in the late morning.

We loved to sleep. He would even sleep under the covers with me. Teddy rarely barked, and the foster mom told me that Trey barked at every noise he heard.

A few weeks later, I met the first dog I would see in person. She was from Puerto Rico, so I called Diana, who is also from Puerto Rico, and she told me that was a sign.

Pepper was the one. She became my next dog. I'm happy that Pepper is also a quiet sleeper. She might even love to sleep more than I do, and I'll hopefully never have a dog that whines to be let outside to pee at five in the morning.

I have learned to live with my grief over losing Teddy. Some days are harder than others, but I deal, just how I live with my mom's death. There hasn't been a day where I don't miss him and his little, white fluffy body. I don't think there will ever be a day when he doesn't pop into my head. I know I gave him the best years a dog can have. That still doesn't make losing him any more bearable.

He should have lived another seven or eight years. He should have been an old man dog. He should have had white, old man hairs spattered into his off-white coat. She took those things away from us. He was the last living thing I had from my mom. So, losing him was like losing her all over again. I think having him with me made her death more bearable. Sort of easier to handle. It was still hard but manageable with him by my side.

I planned to go back up to Arcata to spread Ted's ashes and consciously say goodbye to that place on February 22, 2022. I like it when multiple numbers are in a row, like 11:11 or 5:55. 2/22/22. I went with a best friend of mine, Xenia, who was my former roommate and Teddy's number two.

He loved her so much, and she always cared for him whenever I was unavailable. She also loves numbers and patterns as much as I do. 2/22/22 was even more special being able to share the significance with someone else. It was a beautiful, poetic ending to my very sad story there.

I don't regret going to school there. If I had gone to college somewhere else, I might not have gotten hit by a car. Who knows? Maybe it was so destined that it would've happened wherever I was. It hurts my brain to think in that way. Alternate realities and parallel universes drive me crazy.

Scattering his ashes was cathartic because he deserved to be somewhere beautiful for eternity or whatever, but it was so freaking hard. I was a mess. It was the final goodbye I never got to give him. The final goodbye I never wanted to do or thought I would have to give him so early on in his life.

The lady's insurance company didn't give me much money because she had the bare minimum car insurance you must have to be able to drive. I also got $5,000 for "property damage." The "property" was Teddy.

The fact that they had the gall to give me any amount of money for losing Teddy makes me livid. Angry again that she killed him and furious that her car insurance thought he was worth that little.

Since he was a priceless star, Teddy had won Dog of the Month at my bank up north in August 2019. Just a month before he died. It was a raffle that I entered him in, and he won!

His pictures were probably still up when he lost his little life. We also got treats and a bowl as the rest of his prizes. Who knows where that bowl is now? Long gone, like he is.

A version of me died along with Teddy. I'll never be the person I was the morning of September 7, 2019, ever again.

So innocent and lively. I probably would have changed over the few years I spent healing anyway. I wouldn't have been the same person on September 8th, regardless.

Maybe I wouldn't know all the things medically that I know now. I would have never known about CNS or any of their therapists. I believe that there was a greater reason for this all to happen. For a while, I thought I would get superpowers.

I didn't, though. So, I'm still trying to figure out why it happened to me. I don't think there is an easy answer to *why* it happened. I think it'll prove itself to not just be this horrible thing that happened to me.

In early November 2020, Linda got a five-week-old puppy named Otis. I wanted him to be the first dog I touched after losing Teddy. I was not around any dogs, so he was the first dog I would pet after Teddy's death. Not that I necessarily had the chance to, but I waited until it had been a year since I lost Teddy before I even petted a different dog. Otis was growing in age and size but is forever unbelievably cute.

He came with Linda to pick me up from CNS once a week. I would walk Otis, and we had multiple sleepovers. As we snuggled, he reminded me how much I love dogs. Loving him helped to heal my heart.

No other dog will ever be Teddy, and we'll never have the connection I had with him, but I do have a lot of love that another dog deserves to receive. Teddy became this idea of Teddy though. In my head, he leaped into the perfect memories of Teddy. I only remember all the best things. I have the pictures to help me remember. Entire photoshoots of him looking so incredibly cute in the redwoods, on the beach, on a mountain, or a trail.

I was talking to one of my therapists about my anxiety about getting a new dog. I strongly feared that something terrible would happen to them, too. I also thought I would feel guilty about loving them because they're not Teddy.

She told me about this concept that she read about. My therapist told me the story goes that when you lose something or someone you love dies, there is a hole left in your heart the size of that being.

My next dog will never be Teddy. She'll never be the same size or shape that Teddy was. Pepper and any other dog I have will never fit into the hole he left in my heart. They will never replace Teddy because they can't fit into his hole.

And, I don't want fear to control any aspect of my life. Especially the fear that something terrible could happen to Pepper or any other dog. Adopting her and loving another dog is a little "eff you" to the woman who killed Teddy. I love Pepper differently. My heart will be partially broken forever.

I have two tattoos on my left leg, one is a cartoon of Teddy to commemorate him. I got that one just a week after I got home from the hospital. When I was in the hospital, ever since I found out that Teddy had passed away in our accident, I wanted to get a tattoo of him. I got a tattoo based on a picture of him that I had drawn in a class.

My mom passed away on March 1, 2017. I got the tattoo on February 29, 2020 which any other year would have been March 1, but this year was a leap year, so I treated it as March first to honor them both.

My other tattoo is one that at first was a heart my mom drew on a note to me when she was in the hospital. I got it copied onto my body shortly after she passed away. Then one of my friends turned it into a butterfly. So, every time I see a butterfly I think of mom and my friend fondly.

My counselor at CNS asked me about my tattoos because I have a bunch, and only vaguely remember getting them. When I told her about the ones on my leg, she said it was very symbolic because I was like a butterfly emerging from my cocoon more and more each day.

That was a reminder that mom was looking out for me from wherever in the universe she was. I never believed in heaven before, but that has changed since my accident.

Now, I think my mom is looking out for me. She is next to Teddy, smiling down at me. She must have gotten lonely and wanted him with her. Or maybe she couldn't stop my accident. It had always been written in the stars, so she knew it would happen, and she set me up with my best friend, Teddy.

I know it's unhealthy, but I'm stuck on the *what ifs*.

What if I had left five minutes later?

What if we'd taken a right instead of a left?

What if we'd grabbed a snack halfway through our walk?

What if my roommate had joined us?

These scenarios plague me. They run through my head, driving me crazy. I honestly don't think there was any way to prevent this from happening. It was just some kind of messed up destiny. It's not what I could have done differently. It was what *she* could have done differently.

Teddy was the oat milk in my coffee, the syrup on my pancakes, the hot sauce on my eggs. The peanut butter to my banana. He made everything better. He made me better. More whole. He completed me in infinite ways.

I've felt empty without him. Without my sidekick, my life kind of feels like something is missing. When I got Pepper, the space that he left didn't disappear. It shrank a little, and as she rubbed up next to me, it became easier to handle, but that space would always be empty. My love for Pepper is different. It isn't going to feel the same. She is never going to be Teddy. Or replace him. He is one of my guardians now and wants me to be happy.

i think of teddy
at least a hundred times a day
he was my best friend

chapter 8

did my brain injury make me rude?

will my brain ever
recover inside my skull
who will i be now?

At the start of my recovery, I never said, "thank you" or "please" to anyone, because I didn't know I had to. It's like my brain injury took away all the common courtesy we normally use. I didn't say, "You, too," when people told me to have a good day, but now I do. My first speech therapist, Jackie, worked with me to help me learn what people are supposed to and expected to do.

Diana also worked with me because I never asked anyone how they were or how their day was going. She helped me start asking. At first, she would prompt me to ask her how her day went, until eventually, I initiated it on my own and it became part of what I usually did.

When people told me things about themselves, I first said nothing. When they asked me questions, I answered them but didn't ask any questions back. I didn't know I was supposed to ask questions to keep a conversation going.

My speech therapist at Texhoma made me ask her many seemingly infinite questions. At first, I thought it was very dumb, but it wasn't.

It was to get me used to being interested in other people's lives. I was becoming more polite, more myself. I was learning what people did regularly all over again. Almost like a toddler learning how to exist, but instead, I was *relearning*. Sometimes, I had to ask my aunt if what I wanted to do was rude. She told me that, most of the time, it probably was if I had to ask.

My sense of humor changed after that fateful day, and I lost my empathy for others. For a while, I laughed at things that weren't funny. I laughed when my family friend was telling me about the existence of a home for unwed mothers, when my other family friend told me about her dead dog, and when anyone told me that they were in the hospital or had been in the hospital or were going to go to a hospital.

I laughed when Diana told me she saw dots and threads in her line of sight. Then she said she had to go to an eye doctor and might need surgery. That's when I took it seriously because that meant she couldn't take care of me or drive me around to places. Thank goodness she didn't need surgery.

These days, I have a much darker sense of humor than I used to. I eventually started to get sad when people told me sad things. I began to have empathy for others when, for a while, I hadn't had the capacity to feel that way.

Thank goodness I was capable of being quiet when I saw something sad. I would see sad things and people all the time at CNS, and I became capable of not blurting out anything rude or insensitive.

The coronavirus affected the whole world, especially me because I had to go to rehab on the computer for a few months, which was not nearly as effective as in person. However, when Diana said that most people were in much worse condition and said she wanted to donate to help those in need, I became interested in donating as well.

I was finally thinking of others besides myself. We donated money to World Central Kitchen and Chef Jose Andres, who helped feed people who would otherwise go hungry. Food is a human right and should always be considered as such.

I didn't click with most therapists or the other patients at the hospitals and the nursing home where I was a resident. Part of the reason was that they were so much older than me.

One of my favorite therapists at CNS said something about that time that I found very interesting. She said that maybe I didn't get along with them because my personality was still hidden because of my accident. Maybe that was true, and I didn't get along with them great because I couldn't even understand or make jokes.

Even when I first started at CNS, I didn't smile at anyone or laugh when someone made a funny joke. It took many months to notice that some of my therapists were very funny. I didn't interact with a whole bunch of people besides them because of the coronavirus; because of that, the clinic therapists became some of my closest friends.

They weren't like regular go-out-and-have-fun friends because we worked together. At least, they were my support system at the time.

I also think another part of why I got along with my therapists at CNS better than the ones in the hospital, is that different kinds of people go into different fields. The people working in a hospital setting are either very serious or don't have the time to make a personal connection with their patients.

I didn't ask anyone any questions about themselves for a long time. I couldn't be curious. I didn't have the capacity. Part of that is good because I never wondered, probably out loud, what had happened to other patients I was interacting with in the hospital or any of the houses I was in. So, I never asked.

I realized it is rude to ask someone straight up why they were at CNS. Traumatic brain injuries are often considered "invisible injuries."[8] I do wonder about some of the other patients, people you can't visibly tell what they went through.

When I first made a friend at CNS, Hena, I kept looking at her. You can't tell what happened to her. I had physical and cognitive therapy with her, so she was clearly not functioning at 100%, and so I was curious for a while.

I finally decided to ask. I did it very nicely, starting with, "I hope you don't mind me asking, but …" Hena had had one too many concussions and had been wondering about me, too. I told her that I was unfortunately hit by a car while my dog and I were crossing the street. She asked if that was who I had tattooed on my leg. I replied with yes, always to keep him close to me.

It's weird for me to place myself into my past, even just a few months ago, because things are so different for me now.

---

8   *The invisible scars of brain injuries.* (n.d.). https://www.orlandohealth.com/content-hub/the-invisible-scars-of-brain-injuries/

It's hard for me to even think about the recent past because it seems so far away from where things are now.

Don't even get me started on seeing pictures of myself, especially ones from not that long ago. I feel no kinship with myself in these pictures. I'm not happy this happened to me at all. If I could wish it upon someone else, I wouldn't because it was a horrific experience.

That being said, I think this situation has slowed me down. I ultimately became more understanding and empathetic. Getting hit by a car mellowed me out and probably made me a little funnier. I was funny before, but now I care even less what other people think about what I say.

I was catching up with an old friend who I'd pretty much lost touch with. She recommended that I take mushroom medicinal tinctures. The last time I took a lion's mane tincture was at Texhoma and I had a bad experience with it. I kept thinking (and insisting to everyone) that I had gum in my mouth when I was really creating a sore on the inside of my cheek.

She suggested that I start retaking it regularly anyway and to start leaning into the herbal alternatives to my prescribed medication. In my quest not to be rude or confrontational, I didn't argue with her and also ignored the whole conversation about vaccines. She was strongly against them because she was "strong and healthy." It reminded me that we live in a world of primarily able-bodied people who cater mainly to people who are also able-bodied.

Rehab helped me get back to a semblance of normalcy but I was not about to just take a bunch of herbs and tinctures and ignore science. I am relatively able-bodied. I didn't qualify for another disabled parking pass once mine expired, but I do walk kind of funny, and my right hand is not strong or very coordinated. You can't really tell just by looking at me.

I will continue to try non-traditional forms of healing to complement Western medicine. But I will not rely on them to replace traditional medicine.

After one of my closest friends, Brooke, again suggested a lion's mane supplement when I was visiting her near Sacramento, I told her I wouldn't because of my bad experience. She then suggested taking it in capsule form. I liked that idea.

Using medicinal mushrooms in conjunction with other forms of exercise and brain training. I needed to be open to holistic and scientific communities if I wanted to improve.

she's still in my head
the lady who hit us once
i wish she wasn't

chapter 9

centre for neuro skills before and during a pandemic

here i am alive
living with pain inside me
and so visible

I n late February 2020, almost six months after the car hit us, I was finally out of the hospital system. Because of insurance delays, I was home for about three weeks before I started the outpatient rehab program at CNS, the Centre for Neuro Skills. I don't remember those three weeks, but I liked chilling at home after being hospitalized for six months.

In mid-March I started going to CNS. When I started, I had to use a wheelchair from the parking lot to the building the first couple of days there because it was raining. Everyone was scared that I would fall. I started with going every weekday for six hours, back when they were at their old location. Later, after the pandemic started, they moved to a giant new clinic, and when they reopened, my sessions were reduced to four hours a day.

This way, they could be done before lunch, as they were limiting the number of patients by creating shifts. Thankfully, they were already planning to move when the pandemic started. There was no room for social distancing at the old clinic. The new place always smelled like cleaning solution.

It was an impossibly long journey to be well enough to go to an outpatient, post-acute rehab place like CNS, a six-month journey to be exact. I liked all of my therapists at CNS. They were all so lovely to me. It freaked me out how nice they were at first.

They helped me to start writing with my right hand, and it was there that I took my first solo steps. Very slowly at first because I could only move in what seemed like slow motion. I refused to use any assistive devices. I didn't want a walker or a cane. I would only allow someone to assist me by holding on to the gait belt I had to wear for my safety.

The first week I went to CNS, my family and friends could come in, and we could even leave for lunch. I started at 9 a.m. and left at 4 p.m. After only a few days there, they began to shut down, and they only saw two clients, another patient and me, but we honestly never interacted. We were never in the same therapy at the same time.

It was the beginning of the social distancing, when the coronavirus was just hitting, and affecting the whole world. Causing most of the world to go into lockdown. Thus, CNS couldn't stay open for all the clients.

I was lucky enough to be one of only two patients allowed to attend. I also hated it because I was one of only two people there. It is slightly comforting that the pandemic happened simultaneously with my recovery. It would have been worse if the whole world were going on as it always did, while I was inside, alone with my injury.

I couldn't go to concerts; luckily, no one could go to shows for a while. Society and I were both injured, and we both got better. Societal conventions and I changed because of all this when our whole systems were hugely upset. Hopefully, we will return to normal, or as close to normal as possible. What is normal anyway?

I really liked all my therapists at CNS because they were always looking for ways to challenge me. They tried to make it as fun as possible for me. They were always very positive and hyped me up by constantly praising me. The therapists who I had the best rapport with were my favorites. A few made me laugh the most, and I got very excited to be paired with a few others.

Obviously, my social life was not great because of the coronavirus and my condition. My therapists were the people I was closest to during that time. They were the people I saw the most and were the closest "friends" I had at the time, even though they were getting paid to spend time with me.

We had to stay professional around each other. Also, we could only hang out at the clinic. In any case, I considered them my friends. At least the only option I had.

rehabbing at home

AFTER BEING ONE OF TWO PEOPLE AT CNS FOR SIX DAYS, WHICH felt like six months, they completely shut down. I had to do rehab from home, which sucked because my insurance did not cover rehab on the computer. Tele-rehab was not yet an accepted practice. So, I did not have full six-hour days of rehab while I was at home.

I focused on walking and regaining the use of my hand. I had physical therapy and occupational therapy five days a week each. I also had cognitive rehab three times a week.

CNS also offered educational therapy, but we suspended it for a while because my insurance wouldn't cover tele-rehab at the time and we needed to cut down on the out-of-pocket expenses. My aunt printed math worksheets and comprehension tasks for me to work on for educational rehab, as I was on a limited schedule with CNS.

Diana had been a special education teacher at an elementary school for 15 years, and my understanding at that point was comparable to that of an elementary school-aged child with a learning disability. She became my at-home education rehab specialist and also did extra cognitive exercises with me.

Later, during tele-rehab when PT was on the computer, I did many laps in our living room with my caregiver or aunt supporting me. We worked on my muscle strength using tools like kitchen utensils and small weights we had in the house. When we needed something we didn't have, we ordered it on Amazon.

We even set up my old twin-sized mattress on our living room floor to simulate walking on uneven ground. I did step-ups on it, where I started standing on the ground and stepped onto it. That worked on my leg strength and ability to walk on uneven surfaces. I don't really remember how I felt doing any of this. Probably felt scared that I would fall, then proved myself wrong.

I did ab work along with leg work on that mattress. I did countless crunches and bridges. I did ab work daily, mainly in physical therapy and with my occupational therapists. I wasn't going to have a six-pack, but I do know that a strong core means a stronger body.

I also worked on my posture because it sucked then and posture helps with your balance. When I did laps, I walked backward, forward, and sideways because they all help your brain know how to walk normally.

pandemic therapies

MY THERAPISTS HAD TO GET CREATIVE DURING TELE-REHAB. They would have me do things that didn't require any equipment or used all things just lying around our house. They had me do weight-bearing exercises which are exactly what they sound like. Putting all your weight into your hands or on a certain foot to strengthen them.

I had to move binder clips from one bowl to another. Over and over again. Sometimes from up high or below me. They often had me crossing my midline when I did it. It was tedious but cool to do it and see their reactions to me doing things I couldn't do the week before.

Tina, my main OT, was a therapist who found ways to integrate what I already enjoyed doing, like cooking, with my therapy tasks. She helped us get adaptive tools to make it easier. Cutlery with thicker handles and special cutting boards able to secure food before cutting.

She encouraged us to find ways to work it into my daily life. She also had me practice doing my hair and folding clothes. Regular, seemingly meaningless activities. I had to learn the basics all over again.

In cognitive therapy, we would work on word fluency where I would have to name as many items as possible in one minute that started with a specific letter or fell into a particular category. One day during tele-therapy, my main speech therapist, Victoria, asked me to name the states, and I named 80% more than I usually do because I had learned a song about the states in fifth grade. I remembered it, which is crazy because I don't remember most things, but it stuck with me.

I named the states alphabetically and named more than 30! She and my aunt were stunned. I met the word fluency goal of at least 25 words in one minute in February 2021—almost a year after starting with CNS.

CNS felt like school. Every day the same thing. Some days I felt full of rage for having to be there. When I should have been living my post-college life. I didn't understand why this happened to me when mean assholes could go along through life without getting hit by cars.

It was all a lot of mindless existing. I'd wake up, go to rehab, come home, and wear my splints for a few hours while we watched our TV shows. Dessert was usually in front of the TV so that I could get started earlier with my splints. I felt lonely a lot of the time; it was a very isolating time.

My math and reading skills were affected when my brain was injured. I had tested at a sixth-grade reading comprehension level when I started at CNS but struggled, so they had moved me to third-grade level work. That translated into deficits in understanding and reasoning skills. It was sometimes a mystery to me how my brain got from point A to point B.

While I was at home with Diana and her mom, we watched a lot of TV. It turns out that one thing elderly people have in common with 20-something-year-olds: We both watched a lot of TV.

I remember the hours sitting on the couch with my splints on and how we would have to go through the whole ordeal of taking them off and putting them back on every time I had to go to the bathroom.

We watched at least hundreds, if not thousands, of hours. Days spent on that couch with her mom while Diana offered us snacks, it was a very full-service experience.

After three months of tele-rehab, which felt like at least three years, I went back in person at CNS! On May 26, 2020, we started coming back for in-person sessions. It was the Tuesday after Memorial Day. At first, they only let three people back in, then five, and finally more and more.

CNS re-opens

BEING BACK IN THE CLINIC WAS DISCONCERTING FOR A WHILE and almost surreal. Everyone had to wear masks, and the few times they would touch us, therapists had to wear gloves. Not every therapist was there. Only one or two from each specialty were allowed to be there for the first few months.

Returning to in-person was great, but I hated the masks and shields we had to wear. In the two weeks I was at CNS before the pandemic and throughout tele-rehab, I at least had seen what my therapists looked like.

But because we had to wear masks covering half our faces, I had no idea what the new therapists looked like. The ones that started working after we returned to the clinic. I'd see the new faces for a second if they were taking a sip of something. Otherwise, their noses and mouths were a mystery to me.

We had to wear shields on top of the N95 masks for a few months. It was a little ridiculous. After the therapists and aides were vaccinated in late January and early February 2021, they stopped wearing their shields.

I got my first dose of the vaccine on March 21, 2021. The only side effects I experienced were extreme fatigue for the first day and a sore arm on the side where I got the injection. That lasted only two days, partly because I was stretching and exercising that arm.

My second dose was on the day before my 24th birthday. Shortly after I was vaccinated, I stopped wearing the shield, and I was happy because it was cumbersome.

We continued wearing the N95 mask that they provided every patient. By the middle of June 2021, patients and staff were allowed just to wear surgical masks in the clinic. Outside, though, we got to see each other's faces, so I tried to spend as much time outside as I could.

I had to arrive at 7:50 a.m. for three months. This was so early for me. As soon as I got inside, I would stand by a temperature-checking machine to ensure I didn't have a fever. Then, I had to answer a bunch of questions, even though my answers never changed.

I hadn't had diarrhea recently and hadn't traveled outside the country in the past week. It didn't matter that I went there every weekday, they still asked.

CNS switched back to tele-rehab twice after reopening. Once, right after Thanksgiving to ensure all the patients there would be safe through the winter surge, and another time between Christmas and New Year at the end of 2021 for the same reason. Just for about three weeks in total, which is nothing compared to the almost three months we went on tele-rehab the first time.

working out the kinks

AFTER I WENT BACK TO THE CLINIC, CARDIO WAS EMPHASIZED significantly, which I hated. Cardio and raising your heart rate are beneficial for the brain's recovery because they bring more oxygen into your brain. It was imperative to return to the clinic in person again because they worked me out in the best way. And, the equipment they had was essential to my recovery. We didn't have things like trampolines and balance beams at home!

They made me work hard before when I was working out at home, but the progress was much faster once I went in person again. In physical therapy, I would walk on the treadmill every day.

I wouldn't say I enjoyed it. It was so boring! But walking is the best way to circulate blood flow and oxygen through my body and to my brain.

My team of therapists would have me do other things I couldn't do from home, such as walking on the treadmill with resistance bands strapped around my hips and step ups with weights attached to me.

Alex recommended I do the three flights of stairs up and down to the clinic every day. First with someone to ensure my safety, then doing it alone while holding the handrails, and finally going up and down the stairs completely unassisted. Just one foot in front of the other.

When I first started walking, someone had to hold my gait belt because I didn't have the core or leg strength to hold myself up. I used a gait belt until I did not fall and could walk on my own.

Eventually the gait belt was phased out. I would only use the gait belt when I did certain activities like the "carioca" walking, crossing my feet in front and then in the back of the other one, basically just the grapevine. In physical therapy, we focused on using my right arm and hand, reaching for things with my right hand and picking them from the ground during my walking exercises.

My therapists asked me questions while I did the tasks, which improved my multi-tasking abilities, performing cognitive skills while walking. They also had me do a lot of stretching. So much stretching. We did and I still do the figure-four stretch, where I cross one leg over the other in a figure-four shape and then lean forward. Try it. Really stretches you out.

I began to be able to walk on my own around the house and on my street. It was a huge goal of mine to walk independently. Once I could do that, we didn't need my caregiver anymore, which I had wanted since the day she started working for us. She worked with me for three months.

On her last day in mid-May 2020, I told her I would miss her when she was gone but was not sad to see her go. She said it was good that she was leaving because it meant I was getting that much better.

I was cleared to be independent walking to and from my sessions at CNS on July 21, 2020. They cleared me by having me walk to every location in their building to ensure I knew where I was going. The two main things they had to worry about were me leaving the building or falling.

Both of those were very unlikely. I wouldn't leave because I had nowhere to go. I was even cleared to walk up and down the stairs alone.

My case manager told me the same day I was cleared that it takes some people at least a year to be classified as independent. If they ever make it to that point. It only took me four months because I was motivated.

My answer was always "Yes," whenever they asked me if I wanted to do something longer or harder. Usually, it was "No," when they asked if I wanted a break. I was always very involved with my recovery. I always wanted to know why we were doing something, what it would do for me, and how it would help me in the long and short term.

In occupational therapy, we worked mostly on my right arm and both my hands. My goal was always to use my right hand just as well as I could use my left at the time. It was frustrating to have my right side be more affected. Especially since I am right-handed.

Is this what my life
was supposed to be like?
Is it all chosen?

chapter 10

walking before i could run

all i wanted was
to write a haiku with my
hands and now i have

I had to relearn how to write. Different from when I was five. At first it was with a unique pencil grip. I remember the first time I wrote my first name with my right hand. It was back before the coronavirus, back in the old CNS clinic. I don't know the exact date, but it must have been sometime in March 2020.

My physical therapist gave me a pen. I grabbed it with my right hand and slowly wrote out EMILY OWEN—all caps on a binder that had my home exercise program in it. Before, I had just been using my left hand because, although it was not my dominant hand, it was my least affected hand.

It was a huge accomplishment the day I could write a haiku with my right hand. I practiced writing on my own by writing haiku which has always been my favorite to explain and sum things up.

Using my right hand at that point was like Emily 1.0 using her left hand. Uncoordinated and slow. Various occupational therapists worked on improving my finger dexterity by picking up things, sorting through others, and always crossing my midline.

By late August 2020, I could write without my special pencil grips, sometimes eat a bit with my right hand, and do a successful push-up. I also began writing this book alone.

I did my hair every morning, just a side bun, for months, because that was all I could do for a while. That side bun became a top bun eventually. They may seem like small accomplishments, but to me, they were big.

Cognitive therapy trained my brain to start working the right way again. Cognitive therapy includes speech therapy. We did breathing exercises and read out loud to improve word retrieval, response time, fluency, comprehension, memory, and my ability to stay focused.

Victoria had me work on a cognitive model (the Cog-Mod) that helps develop executive function, word retrieval, processing speed, problem-solving, and thought organization. It's a proprietary therapy strategy developed by CNS.

I had to go through levels of this activity, too. I needed to remember the acronym CSCS WTDF (color, shape, construction, size, weight, texture, detail, and function). I memorized it all quickly because I did it all the time. I needed to organize information about a given item into these eight categories. I will remember CSCS WTDF for the rest of my life.

the sticky issue of insurance

In early 2021, I moved from the CNS day program to outpatient services because nameless people who didn't know me or understand my situation decided what I needed instead of my doctors.

After my insurance company denied me being in the day program, I saw the resident rehab doctor at CNS in October 2020. We needed him to write a letter we could use about why I needed rehab when we filed a grievance to try to get the insurance company to cover the full slate of therapies offered through the CNS day program.

The doctor asked me lots of questions like all the medications I was on and what I thought were the physical impairments I struggled with. I told him that I was just on a muscle relaxer and a low dosage antidepressant.

He had me walk for him, and show him how my right arm doesn't straighten fully. He also asked about the doctors I was seeing. He was very thorough.

We filed a grievance with my insurance company because we believed it was absolutely medically necessary to go to the CNS day program. It was my idea to send them a letter from me the day after they made their decision in order to appeal it. Here is an excerpt from the letter I wrote to them:

> "You make this decision from behind your desks, while I and we are doing the hard work of trying for normalcy. If it wasn't for my resulting injuries and health problems, I wouldn't need CNS. How can you make this decision? This isn't fair to me or the other patients who need them and the services CNS provides.
>
> I strongly urge you to reconsider. This is in fact 'medically necessary' and essential to my recovery. If you could only see my gait,

my right arm, and hear my speech. You would absolutely agree that this is definitely 'medically necessary'. I don't want to be like this for the rest of my life. Their services are a way to sort of right the condition I'm in."

Diana also wrote them a letter on my behalf. She is the one who makes most of my medical decisions. She does a lot of research on all issues and reaches out to friends and experts as needed. Here is an excerpt from her letter:

"Emily's traumatic brain injury in September 2019 was in the form of diffuse axonal injuries. After months in acute care hospitals and nursing homes, she was able to come home and continue her recovery through intensive, targeted rehab at CNS. Emily's TBI left her with spasticity in her right arm, limited range of motion in her right arm and leg, difficulty with balance and walking, and cognitive deficits including memory loss, and visual and speech deficits.

As Emily's brain heals and her body gets stronger and she re-learns skills, she is making improvements every week. She is gaining more independence and increased use of her right side. Now that she has been going in person the services are even more effective.

Emily would not be where she is today without the services and care she receives at CNS. This sudden decision jeopardizes her continued progress and prognosis. The denial must be reviewed with all facts being taken into consideration and a thorough understanding of the services that CNS provides, as it is certainly unique in what it does."

The grievance and appeal were denied.

That meant two doctors had looked at my case and determined that CNS was not medically necessary for me.

That is nuts to me. The health insurance company doesn't care about what level I'm able to read at or how much math I can do.

What they care about is how I'm walking, eating, and sleeping. As far as they're concerned, I have made exceptional progress in the fields they're worried about.

Thankfully, I could afford to privately pay for CNS for a while. If I couldn't and I was just stuck having no rehab for months, this would be unacceptable. It still was unacceptable, but my rehabilitation has never stopped.

We even filed an appeal with the state board for medical insurance to have them decide if my medical insurance should pay. It added insult to my already injured body that I had to prove to all of them that I needed rehab.

No one knew what my future would look like, which was terrifying but realistic. We hired a patient advocate whose job it is to do things like this. She helped us send everything that needed to be sent and do what needed to be done.

The appeal was also denied! So, at the beginning of 2021, CNS formally switched me over from the day program to their outpatient rehab program, hoping that insurance would cover that.

They did, but it wasn't anything like the day program, which was everything, including counseling and educational rehab. I had healed a bunch, not enough for me, but enough for them to stop wanting to pay for the comprehensive day treatment program.

Outpatient covered only physical therapy, occupational therapy, and cognitive rehab. I had already cut down on counseling, so we paid for educational rehab out of pocket. I was only at a 10th grade reading level and middle school-level math according to their tests and needed more time. I had graduated from college, so it was really my ability to stay focused, my processing speed, memory, and attention to detail that was holding me back.

Having a comprehensive program like the one at CNS that included cognitive therapy, counseling and education beyond the basic OT and PT made a huge difference in my recovery. And then you have the other out-of-the-box things like vision therapy, TMS and Botox and custom splints. I know most people don't have access to most of this, so I'm grateful that I did so I could get this far.

talking it out

THE LAST AREA I WORKED ON AT CNS WAS COUNSELING. FOR counseling, I still talked to my therapist from Arcata, which I had been doing since I was able to start talking a little back in December 2019.

For a while, since I already had a therapist, I had stopped doing counseling through CNS, but then in May of 2020, I started EMDR (eye movement desensitization reprocessing) to work on my memory with the CNS counselor.

In those sessions, we talked a lot about the lady who hit me. During those sessions I came to a decision about her. It resulted in my telling the district attorney in my case that I didn't want her to go to jail.

I think the incarceration system in America isn't effective in changing people. I wanted her to do community service instead, working to better the world. In November 2020, I completely stopped going to counseling with CNS.

From then on, I only talked to the same therapist I'd been seeing for five years. She already knew everything there is to know about me, probably more than I do. I was entirely comfortable with her. My mom found her for me when she first got diagnosed, and I have been seeing her since 2016.

walking before I could (try to) run

FOR MANY MONTHS IN SPRING 2021, I WAS TAKING A BIWEEKLY walk around the area surrounding the clinic with one of my PTs, Jellisa. The first time, she told me she would fall back and walk behind me. She wouldn't even let me talk to her initially, which was hard because I love to chit-chat.

When we returned to the clinic, she told me she had been watching for my safety skills. To see if I looked both ways before crossing a street and waited until the crossing sign was lit up before I walked. I wasn't running through the intersections or trying to get my second TBI on a walk with a clinician.

She noted, however, that I didn't look at all before I crossed the street. I just crossed. I realized that I had really come to rely on other people to look for me because there was usually someone with me who would look for us.

We continued these walks for maybe 11 months. I knew they were to test my safety awareness. Still, it took a while for it to become habitual for me. On our last walk-in in late May, she said I was scanning 85% independently. After that, we took a break because we were in Southern California, and after late May it became customary for the temperature to be in the mid-nineties.

One of the first times I worked out with Janki, one of my later physical therapists, she suggested that I work towards running a mile. After I said I didn't plan to run a 5k, I shut down the idea of working towards running a mile one day.

When I tried to "run" the 250 feet that it took to go back and forth down the hallway, I would get winded; I don't have nearly the endurance I used to. I've never been a runner, and I have zero desire to become a runner.

We used to "run" up and down the hallway almost every weekday. Well, for a while, it was me "running." When I first started trying to run again after my accident, Alex was still my physical therapist, I was going very slowly, and she just had to walk, maybe power walk next to me to keep up. Janki loved to push me.

By then I was faster. She would have to jog to keep up with me. She told me I always veer to the right when I "run." At first, I was confused. My right side has always been my more affected side. She explained that I subconsciously fear putting my weight onto that foot because it is my weaker side. So, I put all my weight into my left foot and veer to the right.

Still, I tried running because I wanted to know that I could. We started by breaking down running, which is basically jumping from one foot to the other, over and over again. We practiced the parts of running before trying it again. I worked up a sweat. We were semi-running for so long.

They had a zero gravity machine at CNS. When you're strapped into the machine, it can take off up to 100% of your body weight. The harness is hooked up to a track that runs along the ceiling in the physical therapy gym. I got hooked on it and tried running over the zero-gravity treadmill right under the track.

Janki wouldn't let me try running on the treadmill itself because she said there was no way to stop it if I fell. It took me having to be strapped into a machine on a track over the treadmill for me to be able to actually run.

When you run, there is a moment when no feet are on the ground. Quickly shifting from one foot to the other. I simply did not have the balance to actually run because I was barely moving faster than a typical walk. That's why I couldn't do it on my own. And still can't.

I would be pushing my limits while a therapist casually strolled at my side. But then, I got faster. With time, we would both be power walking.

My brain still hasn't learned how to run, but I've become very good at power walking. Very quickly. It's crazy because I really didn't remember how bad everything had been. How much I had recovered in the previous year. Incredibly, I could now move in a near run, not that fast, but impressive considering I was in a near coma not that long before.

don't call it a comeback

ONE WEEK, CNS HOSTED A PT WEEK CHALLENGE. EACH PAtient had their spot on a poster board. We would get star stickers for completing certain activities. Take a 15-minute walk around the neighborhood or on a treadmill, plank for sixty seconds, wall sit for a minute and a half, walk up and down one of the three flights of stairs, and do thirty sit-to-stand with no hands: one sticker, two, or even five, depending on your chosen activity.

We had a week to win as many stickers as we could. That week, all our PT hours were designated to winning stickers. From the first day, I meant business. I tried winning as many stickers as possible from the beginning, which tapped into the other patients' competitiveness. I did 1oo sit-to-stands in one sitting!

I had 20-something stickers when everyone else had two or three. Then, by day three, I had some real competitors, but I still had the most stickers at the end of the week.

I had 82 stickers, while the guy in second place had 72. There wasn't supposed to be a prize, but my physical therapist brought me a little plastic trophy the following Monday.

Emily 1.0 wasn't competitive but now it means something different. Winning isn't about beating other people, it's about proving to myself that I could do it.

here i am alive
living with pain inside me
still moving forward

chapter 11

tbi's, neuroplasticity, and the power of yet

this here is my life
sometimes i'm not that happy
it is what it is

Brain injuries suck.

Traumatic brain injuries (TBIs) happen about every 11 seconds in the US and Canada.[9] Let that sink in.

That's based on about three million people getting diagnosed every single year. When I read these statistics on the Love Your Brain website, it really shocked me. Not all injuries are reported, so the number is probably higher.

For example, athletes suffer traumatic brain injuries but don't always report them because they want to keep playing the game. No matter what.

---

9   *LoveYourBrain*. (n.d.). LoveYourBrain. https://www.loveyourbrain.com/

Traumatic brain injuries can be caused by a bump, jolt, or blow to your head.[10] You can get one by just bumping your head on something, a seemingly innocent injury. Or you could fall off a ladder, suffer a stroke, be attacked, or get hit by a car (like me). Concussions are the most common type and about 14% of traumatic brain injuries occur from motor vehicle accidents, like the one I was inadvertently involved in.[11]

TBIs are often called a "silent epidemic."[12] The sheer numbers of injuries are scary. So many traumatic brain injuries go undiagnosed and so many people are unaware of their existence. Mainly because the people who suffer from them are walking, talking, breathing, and even driving.

Some people may seem fully recovered when in fact, they are still having a boat load of difficulties. They have cognitive, physical, and emotional deficits as a result of their "invisible" injuries.

If you have a brain injury on the left side of your brain, the right side of your body is more affected.[13] That's because one side of your brain controls movement on the opposite side of your body. Brains are weird like that.

My brain was bruised all over plus the opposite-thing doesn't always apply. For example, neither of my legs worked the way legs should, but my right leg was way more rigid

10   *Get the Facts About TBI | Concussion | Traumatic Brain Injury | CDC Injury Center.* (n.d.). https://www.cdc.gov/traumaticbraininjury/get_the_facts.html

11   TreatNOW. (2020, October 1). *Car Accidents and Brain injury statistics: 2020 - TreatNOW.* https://treatnow.org/knowledgebase/car-accidents-and-brain-injury-statistics-2020/

12   *Traumatic Brain Injury: A "silent epidemic" | Center for Brain Injury and Repair | Perelman School of Medicine at the University of Pennsylvania.* (n.d.). https://www.med.upenn.edu/cbir/silentepidemic.html

13   *Brain anatomy and how the brain works.* (2021, July 14). Johns Hopkins Medicine. https://www.hopkinsmedicine.org/health/conditions-and-diseases/anatomy-of-the-brain

than my left. That prevents me from having a "normal" gait when I walk.

I knew I wore my splint on my right leg, but I always thought both legs weren't working properly. One day, I was walking on the treadmill at CNS, and I realized only my right knee wasn't listening. Since I have a brain injury, I don't know whether my right leg will always and forever be my bad leg. All I knew was that I had to do everything possible to improve it.

I used to fear never healing and never getting any better. I thought I would be in and out of hospitals for the rest of my days. Back when I was still in the hospital, I bet against myself. I bet Linda that I wouldn't walk independently for at least five years. I didn't believe in myself.

In March 2020, only about six months after my accident, I paid my debt. Not even close to five years, so that tells you how "optimistic" I was in my prediction of how my recovery would go. I told her that I would happily pay.

I also made a bet against Diana that I would never live independently again. Instead of giving her money, I promised to take her to a nice dinner when I was officially discharged from CNS.

She has been integral to my healing process. She was there the day after our accident in Northern California when I was in a near coma. She came to see me in the hospital almost every day for the five and a half months I was there. She drove me to and from rehab every day for months and months.

Both of them made these bets against me because they were so confident in me, so confident they would win, and that I'd be more mobile than I expected.

All my therapists, especially the occupational ones, would tell me to cross the midline and explained this means reaching across the middle of my body with arms or legs and doing things on both sides, not just the affected side. They told me that's because doing things on the "better" side of your body teaches your brain what it should feel like on the not-so-good side. So, eventually, both sides can hopefully be working at the same level. It strengthens the connections between both sides of your brain and helps you use both sides of your body together.

I have also used a mirror as another attempt to trick my brain. Seeing the mirror image of my left hand completing exercises tricked my brain into thinking my right hand was actually completing them successfully. Turns out, our brains are surprisingly easy to trick.

Neuroplasticity describes the ability of the brain to change in response to the input it gets. "Use it and improve it" is something Tina used to tell me.

I am recovering because all brains have neuroplasticity. She taught me all about it and about how repetition, intensity and age all matter with a long PowerPoint presentation and even gave me a research article by neuroscientists Jeffrey Kleim and Theresa Jones to educate me on the principles guiding neuro rehab.[14]

Basically, when you do something over and over again, you grow new pathways between your neurons, and the repetition strengthens the connections between the neurons in your brain. You can train yourself to perform a specific function by doing it a lot.

---

14   Kleim, J. A., & Jones, T. A. (2008). Principles of Experience-Dependent Neural Plasticity: Implications for Rehabilitation After Brain Damage. *Journal of Speech, Language, and Hearing Research, 1*, 227–229. https://doi.org/10.1044/1092-4388(2008/018)

To make something new stick in your brain, you need to do it the right way repeatedly. Even if you have done it a million and one times before your injury. After you suffer a brain injury, you have to do something as basic as walking a ton of times for your brain to really know how to do it again.

The concept that your brain can get progressively better and heal by regrowing connections, and sometimes even neurons, is relatively new. Before, people thought the wiring in your brain was fixed and that neurons and connections were gone forever once lost.[15] Thankfully this isn't true. Or else I would have lived my whole life not being able to walk, spending decades in a bed.

I've even heard from some of my older therapists that when they were in school, they were taught that after any kind of injury, the brain stayed stagnant. My life has continued to get better and will continue to get better because of neuroplasticity.

"Repetition, repetition, repetition" became my mantra. My OT explained that a person whose brain is disrupted must do something at least 400 times to teach the brain how to do it properly again. "Neurons that fire together, wire together."[16] This and other concepts from neuropsychologists like Donald Hebb describe how pathways in the brain are created and reinforced through repetition.

15   UNESCO International Bureau of Education. (2021, June 28). *IBE — Science of learning portal — Neuroplasticity: How the brain changes with learning*. IBE — Science of Learning Portal. https://solportal.ibe-unesco.org/articles/neuroplasticity-how-the-brain-changes-with-learning/

16   Neuroscience News. (2021, December 23). *How neurons that wire together fire together*. https://neurosciencenews.com/wire-fire-neurons-19835/

The brain adapts to the world it is experiencing. We can help it do that with repetition and hard work. As I've been told countless times, "You can train your brain."[17]

Connections may not be able to regrow or grow as you get older. Age does matter. The whole time I was in a near coma, every doctor told my family that I would likely recover because I was only 22 when I was injured.

However, they couldn't tell them when or even if I would wake up from the minimally conscious state, which is the term they used instead of saying "coma." They just all said *probably*.

For example, I reacted to discomfort and pain; my legs moved crazily, and I squeezed people's hands. At one point, one of my doctors was even preparing Diana and advising her about the possibility that we would have to prepare for the financial burden of caring for someone in that condition for life and looking into a suitable facility for me.

When you lose one sense, your other senses may become stronger. This amazing adaptive feature of the brain is called cross-modal plasticity.[18] I'm no doctor, but my hearing is extra sensitive post-accident to overcompensate for other things I've lost.

There are ways to increase neuroplasticity in your brain. That's why I went to rehab. My therapists explained that through physical exercise, you can create new blood vessels and neurons. You increase and reinforce neurons and synapses in your brain through cognitive exercises.

---

17   Harvard Health. (2021, February 15). *Train your brain.* https://www.health.harvard.edu/mind-and-mood/train-your-brain
18   Rabinowitch, I., & Bai, J. (2016). The foundations of cross-modal plasticity. *Communicative & Integrative Biology, 9*(2), e1158378. https://doi.org/10.1080/19420889.2016.1158378

I was constantly yawning during cognitive rehab and counseling when we were working on my memory. My counselor said I was inadvertently trying to oxygenate my brain while doing the things that would make me heal faster. I yawned all the time. I don't think I did before my accident. I was convinced it was a sign of my brain craving more oxygen than it was getting regularly.

You also need to avoid stress, especially after an accident, because it increases a hormone in your body that is bad for recovery. How hard you work also affects your ability to heal. During your rehabilitation process, your body will change. When you learn something in one setting, you can learn to transfer that learning to another setting, generalizing it. When an injury occurs, the brain adapts and uses things you have learned in a different way than it was learned originally. The brain wants to heal.

I talked much slower than I used to because my lung capacity was low and my mouth muscles were significantly weaker. So, my speaking pace was not very fast anymore. I used to talk a mile a minute, very fast, and suddenly I had to slow down noticeably to be fully understood.

I did sustained phonation in cognitive rehab, which is a fancy name for speech therapy. This is where I said AHHH for as long as I could. When I started with CNS, I could only hold my AHHH for seven seconds. As of June 2021, I could hold it for around nineteen seconds. The goal for a woman is between fifteen and twenty-five seconds. I thought holding it out for six more seconds was crazy, but I kept saying, "I'm just not there yet," until I was.

I didn't just give up and accept that my right hand couldn't work well or that I couldn't walk correctly. I worked to change it.

Diana was a special education teacher who used to teach her students the importance of living life with a "growth mindset" (the belief that you can develop your abilities and learn new things through practice and hard work) and believing in the "Power of Yet" (the concept that you may think you cannot do something now, but it's really just that you can't do it yet), concepts taught and pioneered by Carol Dweck, a leading psychologist in this field.[19]

My aunt explained these concepts to me. Never accepting stagnation, working towards change. Understanding that I could change my own future empowered me through a time when my future was a question mark.

When I was minimally conscious, my aunt kept reminding herself that my brain wasn't ready to wake up YET. That gave her hope. The brain can change or rewire the connections between its neurons. Just because you cannot do something now doesn't mean you won't ever be able to. You just can't do it YET.

I operated under the belief that I simply couldn't do the things I wanted to YET but would be able to in the future. It just took lots of hard work and dedication to improve myself. Or at least what you hope that better version will be. Rebuilding the connections in your brain is why people with TBIs need rehab and why it worked for me.

every day I

see people much worse off

I guess I'm lucky

---

19   Dweck, C. (2014 B.C.E., October 9). *Developing a Growth Mindset* [Video]. www.youtube.com.

chapter 12

out of the box

the sun and the moon
i guess i'm seeing in two
double negative

To answer the question mark that my life has become, I'm up for trying new things that might help. Also, a disclaimer I should include: never try anything without consulting your doctor or a medical professional.

I'm open to any and all options, but only after I've run it by my neurologist first. If I can be part of research that will ultimately help people who get hit by cars know where to go and what to do after their accidents, I will gladly help. I am still considered a guinea pig for many things.

While the focus has been and will be on traditional treatments and therapies, I am also open to holistic remedies like lion's mane mushroom tablets and various herbal supplements. I also tried other non-traditional things, so I'll describe them here in case they can help.

transcranial magnetic stimulation

IN LATE SEPTEMBER 2020, I TRIED TMS (TRANSCRANIAL MAG-
netic stimulation).[20] We had met a neurologist at UCLA
through one of Diana's friends. He is the one who advised
my aunt at the beginning of all of this and who had looked
at all my brain scans. When less than a year later we did a
Zoom consultation, he was surprised by my progress.

Not to brag, but my progress has been very unexpected
and off the charts. He put me in contact with another UCLA
doctor who recommended TMS, usually used to fight depression. They were interested in doing some tests to see if it
would help treat cognitive deficits in traumatic brain injury
patients.

This is considered an off-label treatment. I was one of
their lab rats. It was experimental. There had been little research on this because it was so cutting-edge. One of the few
studies on this issue showed no cognitive improvement, but
was done with patients with more severe TBI's, and with a
median Glasgow Coma Scale (GCS) of around 3 or 4.[21] My
GCS was a nine at admission but dropped to a five during
later testing. By the time we tried TMS, I scored 15, the highest score.

I figured if it couldn't hurt me, why not try it. They had
successfully helped fight anxiety and depression with TMS,
and those people seemed to do better cognitively, making
them think that it could help with traumatic brain injuries.
I was lucky enough to get this opportunity, I figured I might

20   Durbin, K. A., Marder, K. G., Wilson, A., et al., (2023). Low frequency transcranial magnetic stimulation for cognitive recovery after traumatic brain injury: A case
report. *Psychiatry Research*, 2(2), 100173. https://doi.org/10.1016/j.psycr.2023.100173
21   Lee, S. A., & Kim, M. (2018). Effect of Low Frequency Repetitive Transcranial Magnetic Stimulation on Depression and Cognition of Patients with Traumatic Brain
Injury: A Randomized Controlled Trial. *Medical Science Monitor*, 24, 8789–8794. https://
doi.org/10.12659/msm.911385

as well try and who knows, maybe this could end up helping others.

They decided on a type of TMS that minimized the risk of seizures. They were tapping on the right side of my brain to quiet it down. They hoped that by quieting down the right side of my brain, the left side, which is the side struggling more, would be forced to work harder. Compensation.

For the two weeks I did their program, I went to CNS later in the day than I had been. I started out every day that I was doing the TMS followed by cognitive rehab at CNS because, hopefully, the tapping would have primed my brain to benefit more from the rehab.

The first day that I participated in TMS, they had me take a bunch of cognitive tests. Then the next day, I started doing the actual TMS. It took between 20 and 40 minutes and felt like a woodpecker pecking on my skull. Before starting it, they wanted to test my brain's sensitivity. So, they hooked me up to something that made my fingers move involuntarily.

After two weeks of tapping, I had more cognitive testing to see if their plan was actually working. They had me listen to a set of words and then tell them all the words I could remember, showed me a picture and then twice had me draw the picture from memory, and listen to a story I had to tell back to them at least once after doing another activity.

I often wonder how I would have done on these tests before my brain injury. Or how anyone else would do.

They also did an EEG after my brain was tapped for two weeks. Based on their testing, I significantly improved my attention and working memory. Before I started the TMS, the cognitive testing in this area concerned remembering number sequences, and the resulting information placed me in the 37th percentile.

This means I scored higher than 37 percent of people and lower than 63. After I completed just two weeks of TMS, that number moved to 91! So, I did better than 91 percent of people and worse than nine percent.

My executive functioning in one test went from the 16th to the 50th percentile. Executive functioning means my ability to organize, plan, and prioritize. It is also responsible for paying attention, regulating emotions, and self-monitoring. Not all my results were that dramatic, but in most areas my testing showed improved skills, and only a few stayed the same or went down.

I got a second EEG after my two weeks with them were up. It showed that the left side of my brain was working much harder after the tapping. That was exactly what they had wanted it to do. The results showed that before TMS, my brain waves had the same intensity as they would when I was sleeping.

After TMS, that low rate of activity was gone. The rate of brain waves in the right side of my brain, which controls executive function and attention, increased after TMS.

Basically, after TMS, my brain on the EEG looked more "normal." I didn't know definitively that TMS helped me, or maybe rehab was really helping me, or just the passage of time and more healing, but it was worth it to do more.

So, I went back for another two weeks of tapping a few months later. They didn't know what the implications of time would be. They felt confident about the improvement because I was simultaneously doing supplementary cognitive rehab with CNS. That was why I waited a few months before I went back in.

My results were so noteworthy, the UCLA team asked for my consent to write a paper for a medical journal about my experience as a TBI patient. As I read it, I realized the type of TMS I did was actually called rTMS (repetitive transcranial stimulation). It was published in August 2023.

botox

ANOTHER OF WHAT I CONSIDER "OUT OF THE BOX" TREATMENT was using Botox to loosen my muscles. I went to my neurologist for mega shots to my right hand, forearm, and pecs to treat the spasticity (for me it presented as tightness) on my right side.

When we hear Botox, we think of wrinkles. But in February 2020, I got Botox injected in my right arm and pec for the first time at my last hospital. I remember my ex-girlfriend had been over to bring me dinner after we had waited for the doctor all day.

She was there when the doctor came by and held my hand tightly while I was stuck with the huge needle. You can get Botox every three months, so after I left the hospital and it was time for me to get my second injection, we decided to continue seeing the same neurologist.

The shots really helped me because, before that, I couldn't open my hand or stretch my arm out. My hand was always clenched in a claw, I couldn't raise my arm, and it was stuck bent at my elbow. After Botox, I started to be able to write with my right hand, brush my teeth, hold a glass, and finally switch from dictating to typing this book on my own in the Summer of 2020.

I got around six times as much as people cosmetically get in their face. It also goes straight into my muscles that need loosening up.

It usually takes one to two weeks to tell a difference from the medication. However, the first time I was injected, the results were so quick that my neurologist and the hospital rehab doctor were surprised at the effects.

After the first injection though, it took longer to see the results from the other shots. For many months, my right arm still couldn't fully straighten out. It became more comfortable to be slightly bent at the elbow, which is what the muscles in my arm were most comfortable doing.

But my hand was doing so well that my neurologist didn't want to give me any more Botox in my forearm. She said that therapy would be enough.

I got my fourth Botox shot in early November 2020. It went straight into my bicep and my pec muscles, and it hurt so much. Those were my tightest spots. It was another turning point.

That night was the first night in almost a year that I didn't wear the thing strapped to my arm to keep my arm from retracting. I slept like a baby. All curled up on me with my arms folded under my head. It was such a relief.

I've never experienced happiness while asleep before this. In the beginning of December 2020, my arm could straighten out fully. I was officially declared *within normal limits* when straightening out my arm.

My muscles still aren't used to this new positioning, though, so it isn't always straight. My arm sometimes bends at the elbow, especially when I'm sleepy and not paying attention.

hyperbaric chamber

IN FEBRUARY 2022, I STARTED GETTING AN HOUR AND A HALF OF oxygen therapy. It's called a hyperbaric chamber, and you're in a small pod pumped full of pure oxygen. You're wearing an oxygen mask and breathing pure oxygen for the 90-minute session. I tried the hyperbaric chamber after my dad suggested I try it.

His best friend and business partner had suffered a stroke during my recovery and had gotten a personal hyperbaric chamber for his house. He suggested I come try it. After consulting with my neurologist, being instructed not to try one in someone's home, and a lot of research to find the right place, Diana found a facility close to CNS' old location.

Hyperbaric chambers are thought to reduce spasticity, increase the oxygen going to your brain, and reduce any leftover inflammation in my brain.[22] Some use it to treat veterans with PTSD and TBIs.[23] It is mostly used to treat decompression sickness, burns, wound treatments, and serious infections.[24] Recent studies suggest they can help improve cognition impairment.[25]

Health insurance covers a few uses, mostly the ones that speed up the healing of things like tissue damage. But my treatment wasn't covered. The place my aunt found almost guaranteed me that I would notice a difference in my speech and that it would reduce any inflammation in my brain.

---

22   *Neurological Conditions | Hyperbaric Centers of Texas*. (n.d.). Hyperbaric Centers of Texas. https://www.hyperbariccentersoftexas.com/conditions-treated-hbot/neurological-conditions/
23   Meshad, S. (2022, February 16). *Hyperbaric Oxygen Therapy (HBOT) effect on PTSD and TBI*. National Veterans Foundation. https://nvf.org/ptsd-tbi-and-hbot/
24   Office of the Commissioner. (2021, July 26). *Hyperbaric oxygen therapy: Get the facts*. U.S. Food And Drug Administration. https://www.fda.gov/consumers/consumer-updates/hyperbaric-oxygen-therapy-get-facts
25   Gottfried, I., Schottlender, N., & Ashery, U. (2021). Hyperbaric Oxygen Treatment—From Mechanisms to Cognitive Improvement. *Biomolecules, 11*(10), 1520. https://doi.org/10.3390/biom11101520

They recommended that you complete forty 90-minute sessions, totaling 60 hours.

I always had a piece of gum to chew for when my ears started popping. Mint, fruit, or cinnamon. I usually chose mint or maybe cinnamon. Fruit gum is gross.

It's so boring lying in the pods. No electronics are allowed, so no phones. I usually used that time as my reading time. I read four books in the sixty hours I spent there. Some days, I would watch a TV show or a movie on their iPad that was Velcro-ed to the window so you could see it.

I love to read. I've always loved to read. I used to win the reading competition my elementary school had for the most pages read each month. Now, I'm a much slower reader.

I don't know why because it feels like I'm reading at the same speed I've always been reading at, but now it'll take me more than a few sessions to finish a short book. It's hard to tell how much the hyperbaric treatments helped me, but more than a few people commented on how my speech had improved after the recommended 40 sessions.

sometimes you do have to learn how to ride a bike again

On June 24, 2022, I started a new program with a group called the Cognition Center, a pair of therapists who come to your house. My neuro-optometrist told me about them after I failed my driving assessment.

The Cognition Center comprises two people; an occupational therapist, Cristin, who used to work at CNS and was a brain injury survivor herself, and her partner/former bike racing coach, Ron. Our first two sessions were an hour long and focused on getting to know me. Then we transitioned to 90-minute sessions, with the end goal being to improve my balance, focus, planning, problem solving and multitasking through being able to ride a bike again.

I started with a bike that had no pedals, but it still had wheels. I ran through our neighborhood with it between my legs. Over and over again. Up and down my street. They told me running a bike without pedals would help my walking gait and help prepare me for when I graduated to pedals.

I graduated to pedals faster than they expected. Four weeks in and I convinced them to start me on the traditional bike. At first I needed to have a finger touching my back while one of them ran alongside me. Then on our fourth session of me asking to take off the proverbial training wheels, I was allowed to ride the real bike. With pedals.

At first, I was only allowed to bike very short distances on our street with them both watching me closely. Then I graduated to whole stretches of the streets in my neighborhood with someone running alongside me, then with someone biking in front or behind me, and finally with someone riding in front of me and someone riding next to me.

To get me ready for riding, I had to multitask and stay focused on riding in the middle of the street. Other times, I would have to spot every letter of the alphabet, either on license plates or street signs or on the signs hung up restricting dog's potty areas and redirecting parking. Sound familiar? At CNS doing exercises with distractors was one of the final stages in my program.

Cristin and Ron also helped me work through other parts of my life I needed help with besides just helping me with the underlying skills needed to relearn to ride a bike. One of them was helping me understand I needed more rest to let my brain heal and recharge.

I get so exhausted easily, not just tired, but genuinely exhausted. Life takes it out of me these days and I can't function as spontaneously or effectively as I did before my accident. I sleep more and drink coffee more often. I've never gotten a clear answer on whether coffee is bad for the brain-injured population.

I know other brain-injured folks who even shy away from coffee. I don't necessarily remember how caffeine used to affect me, but I know how it affects my new brain. At least how it makes me feel, not necessarily what damage it is doing to my brain; but just in case, I try to limit myself to one-maybe one and a half cups of coffee a day.

I told Cristin and Ron about my exhaustion and constant sleepiness, and they suggested daily naps. Since I got that tip, I try to squeeze in a nap almost every day from 3:33 to 4:20, an hour and 11 minutes; 111. To stay in one of the themes in my life.

they couldn't tell me
when/if I would get better
writing my story

chapter 13

cooking & eating

i never forgot
what foods went well together,
my brain works weirdly

'm fairly plant-based in my eating habits; no dairy, limited cheese, and only eggs that come from chickens who eat plants so to me, they're plant-based. I forgo the meat and the whole milk creamers both for the planet and for my own morals/body. I am primarily a vegetarian and have been since my freshman year of college.

Basically, everyone at Humboldt was something other than a carnivore, and I am easily convinced. It was and still is something I have always stood by. What gives us the right to torture, kill, and eventually eat other living creatures? Just because we think they taste good?

When I couldn't advocate vegetarianism while I was minimally or barely conscious, I had external advocates looking out for me. Diana insisted that the food supplement pumped into my tummy through a tube be organic and mostly vegetarian. Later, others insisted on veggie burgers and meatless sausages when I couldn't.

I could only eat soft foods that required no chewing when I first started eating real food. I was still gaining control over my muscles, and my mouth muscles weren't strong enough to chew yet. I had to use a straw when I first started drinking water for two reasons.

First, they didn't want me to choke by taking too big gulps or for the liquid to go down into my lungs because when that happens, you can get pneumonia. Second, neither of my hands was strong enough to hold onto a cup.

I couldn't feed myself during the first months of my hospitalization because neither my arms nor hands were strong enough to hold anything. While restricted to soft foods, I ate a lifetime supply of applesauce 10 times over.

One of the first times my aunt fed me some applesauce, she went to the kitchen for a few minutes to ask a question, and while Diana was gone, I picked up the applesauce container and started drinking it. That was the first time I fed myself after our accident.

From the beginning, I didn't like always relying on another person for tasks I used to do myself. I literally had to take matters into my own hands.

On Thanksgiving, I decided to eat my pumpkin pie first, because when you just start eating real food after two months of being fed intravenously, it's totally ok to eat dessert before dinner.

After that, I ate three servings of mashed potatoes and cranberry sauce. Still, I was hungry. That's because I didn't know what hunger felt like. I was just so excited to eat real food that I thought I was hungry any time I wanted food.

My favorite thing to say was "MORE!" I didn't have any impulse control at the time.

My grandpa and his wife, Judi, came to visit over the holidays. One of the most vivid memories I have from my recovery was her patiently helping me to feed myself. It was sitting with her when I first held a fork and put the bites in my mouth for the first time in months.

She wasn't putting the fork into my mouth; she would hand it to me after putting some food on it. I finally could feed myself, not just be fed.

One of the things I now have to learn to work on because of the TBI is, and maybe always will be, my impulse control. The TBI destroyed my ability to control my impulsivity. It became a constant struggle.

It was always in the back of my head as something I was dealing with. Although I think that even having the awareness that I am now prone to impulsivity kind of counterbalances it.

Whenever anyone came to see me, I would look to see what they brought me. I became so used to everyone bringing me food. One week, I asked everyone who came to see me for french fries, and they had all brought me french fries. I ate french fries probably six times that week.

Then, my aunt instituted a healthy food policy. People couldn't just bring me junk food.

One of my mom's friends came to the kitchen at Texhoma to make pizza with me! She brought dough, cheese, vegetables, and sauce so we could assemble our own. My mom's other friend made me peanut noodles and brought me food from a local restaurant.

In late December 2019, I made chocolate chip blackberry jam cookies (from a recipe that had come from my own brain years before) with my occupational therapist and latkes with my dad. That brought cooking into my recovery.

I started small, helping Mike, my dad, and eventually Diana with cooking duties. I went through the tiers toward independently cooking and baking in the kitchen.

When I was moved from Texhoma to Northridge Hospital, my family and friends continued to bring me food. It became necessary because the hospital food service was not the best.

Once, they said they would give me a veggie burger and french fries, but they only sent french fries along with all the fixings for a burger—ketchup, lettuce, and pickles on the side. My ex-girlfriend and our mutual best friend were visiting and had to go get me a burrito to satisfy my hunger.

For a long time, I thought I'd lost my ability to make up delicious recipes on the fly. With no recipe or instruction, simply feeling it out. Tasting as needed. For years, I had cooked by feeling, without a recipe.

Only in October 2020, more than a year after our accident, did I trust myself to cook without a recipe again. Mostly soups, elaborate salads and sandwiches, a stir fry, or even just well-spiced or glazed roasted veggies with a grain or carb, things that are very hard to mess up.

It took me about three months to trust that I still had *it*. The power to cook and trust that it would taste good when it was done. It turned out, I didn't lose my ability to cook off-the-cuff. Without a recipe, just cooking. I wonder if my food still holds a candle to my old cooking.

After getting hit by a car, I based my cooking off of recipes most of the time. I would feel for how the veggies wanted to be cooked. It took me a while to get there.

By July 2022, I was baking cakes and cookies for my therapists on birthdays. I was put in charge of cooking for Meatless Mondays in my house.

I love to cook. Not to humbly brag, but cooking has always been a skill of mine. I understand flavors and how they taste together. My life's goal used to be to have a farm-to-table food truck with my garden attached.

For years, that is what I was striving towards and working towards. Then a car hit me and changed my life's plan.

Maybe in some alternate reality, I do have that food truck, but now the idea seems like too much pressure, and the thought of it makes me nauseous. I feel like I have more important things calling my name now. I think cooking is a great way to go about helping to save the world, but now I'm headed toward writing my book and being a kind of motivational speaker.

I know I will always love cooking, it will forever be close to my heart, but more of cooking as a hobby rather than a career. I'm learning that doing something you love for your main money-making job might ruin it for you.

Cooking is not something I ever want not to enjoy doing. I can escape into it regardless of the stresses in my life.

food makes me happy
there's not a lot that does now
so i cling to it

my first (and hopefully last) private jet ride! eureka—> los angeles
Photo credit: John Owen

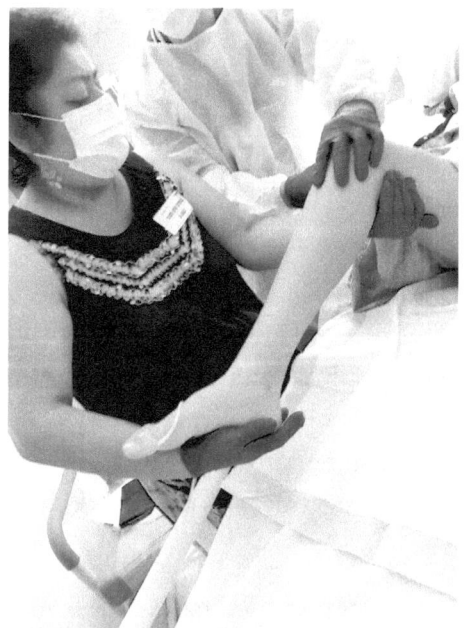

my childhood nanny doing range of motion exercises with my
minimally conscious self at barlow
Photo credit: Diana Rivera

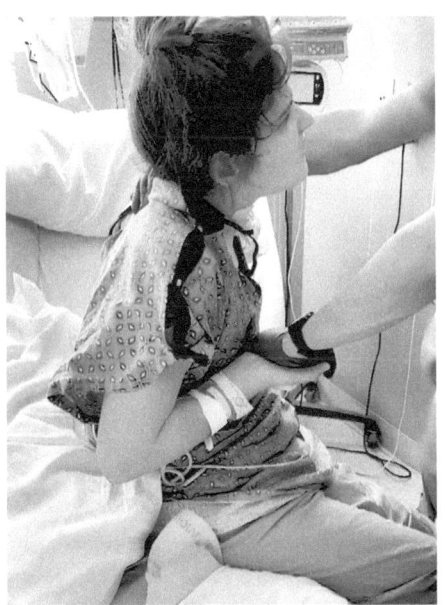
the first time i sat up at barlow after lying down for six whole weeks
Photo credit: Diana Rivera

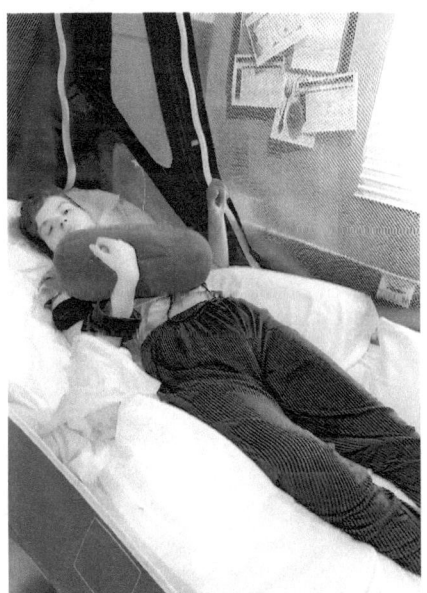
this was the posey bed at texhoma I would get zipped
into for my safety
Photo credit: Diana Rivera

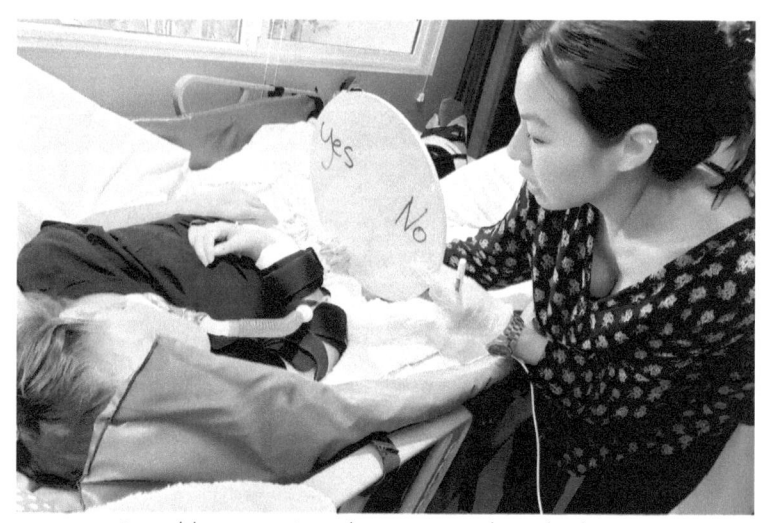

i would communicate by pointing when i hadn't yet
relearned how to speak
Photo credit: Linda Sutton

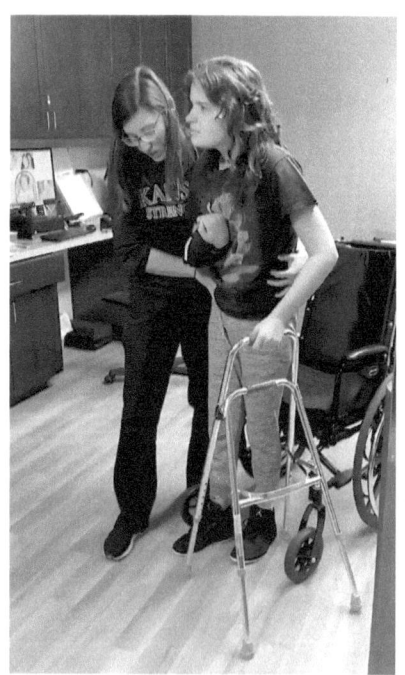

learning to walk at texhoma with assistive devices i
would later refuse
Photo credit: Diana Rivera

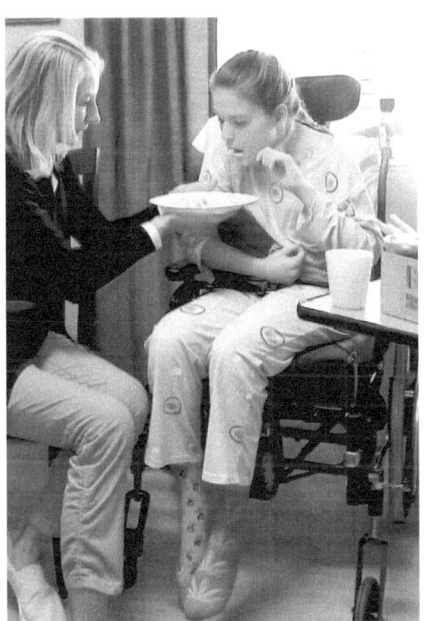

being taught how to eat with a fork again
Photo credit: Diana Rivera

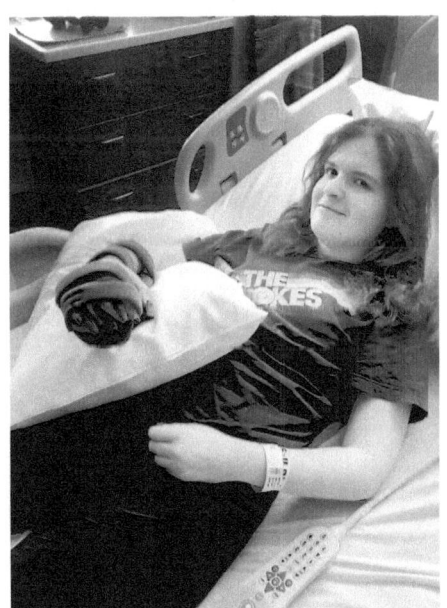

lying at northridge hospital wearing one of the splints i used to
wear to help me extend my limbs fully
Photo credit: Diana Rivera

walking into the house after living in different medical
facilities for six months
Photo credit: Linda Sutton

during telerehab we had to set up a gym in our living room
Photo credit: Diana Rivera

the first time i walked independently
Photo credit: Guillermina Pila

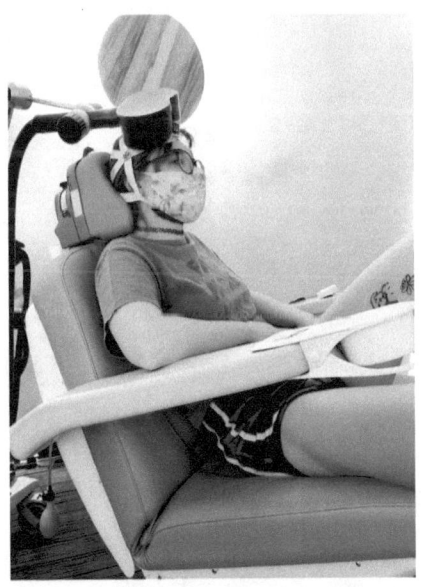

transcranial magnetic stimulation tapping
treatment at ucla
Photo credit: Diana Rivera

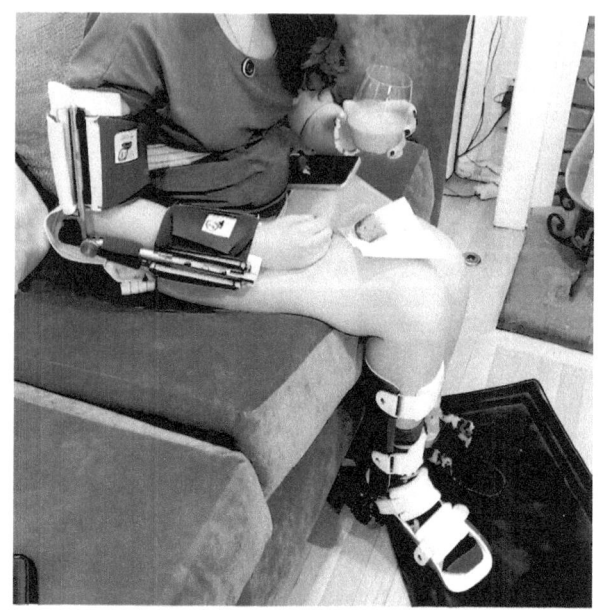

i hated the dynasplints but they did their job
Photo credit: Diana Rivera

one of the seemingly infinite sunsets i saw with teddy in Humboldt
Photo credit: Logan Brown

chapter 14

advocating for myself

she just left the bar
it was written in the stars
her car hit me hard

I finally started to have a say about things when I was at Northridge Hospital. They took so much blood out of my body. Every day, a few vials. Over and over. Probably gallons of my blood. A nurse would come into my room daily for weeks and draw blood.

Until one day, I said no.

Told them they couldn't take any of my blood. I simply refused. The nurse who had come in to take my blood just left. They just left when I refused. I had power—more than I'd had in months.

I felt drunk with power. They didn't have a rebuttal to give me. They just walked away when I said I didn't want them to take my blood.

Then, when Diana came later that day, they told her what had happened. When she heard, she explained that they had to take my blood because that was how they discovered what they needed to know about me and how to treat it.

I never refused a blood draw after that explanation. I just needed to be given a reason, an acknowledgment of some control over what happened with my body.

I was against unnecessary treatments or anything that was not an efficient use of time at CNS. For example, during my OT sessions, my therapist would have me stare at a light with different colored lenses for twenty minutes. It was called light therapy. My neuro-optometrist prescribed it to help align my eyes.

I felt like it was a waste of my time at CNS to do it for the length of time he wanted me to do it. It was boring, and I needed no support or supervision. I just sat there. I hated it. It lasted twenty minutes, while I was only at CNS for two to three hours.

So, I asked my aunt to call my neuro-optometrist's office and ask whether I could get the lenses and the special light bulb at home instead. They responded that most people did it at home anyway. I was no longer wasting my time on it during my limited time for occupational therapy at CNS.

I've had to do light therapy multiple times during my recovery. Sometimes for twenty minutes. Others for just four minutes. Sometimes with different colored lenses and others with just one color. But I did it the way I wanted to do it.

In October 2020, I was still receiving counseling twice a day at CNS. Sometimes two of my three hours at CNS would be spent in counseling when I could barely write or walk independently. Once alone and once in a group. The group would be a young people's group to help with our social skills.

Even though I've become very self-centered—after all, the world seemed to revolve around me while I was hospitalized and while I was at the residential facility—I think my social skills are one of the things that haven't changed much because of my injuries.

I am still chatty, very funny, and can converse with anyone. However, I've lost my impulse control and filter, and it isn't always pleasant for those on the receiving end when I want something or am upset by something.

A few other young patients couldn't converse with you. Some of them couldn't even make eye contact with you. It's probably partially that they were not cognitively able to talk freely with other people or maybe were shy in a new place. In any event, I didn't think it would be very beneficial for me.

I wanted to be proactive, always working to improve cognitively and physically. So, I talked to my case manager and explained my situation. She switched me out of my second counseling session.

When it was clear that I would come home from the hospital, Diana wasn't sure where I would sleep. At first she thought I would sleep in a hospital bed in the corner of her room.

I quickly nixed that idea. I had slept in a hospital bed for five-and-a-half months. I wasn't going to do it at home.

I insisted on a regular bed just two days before I came home. So my aunt had to scramble to locate and buy me a bed and to find rails for it so I wouldn't fall out of bed.

Our family friend found the bed at a mattress store near our house, and it was delivered to our house within the day. I needed to assert myself or I would have been sleeping in yet another hospital bed, and it wouldn't feel like I was finally moving on.

When I know what I want, I push and push until I'm ready for it. Those powers of manifestation were turned towards my injury; it worked in my favor most of the time.

While I was sleeping on that twin bed in the corner of Diana's room, I wanted to move and sleep in my own bed in my own room. However, it wasn't safe for me to do that yet. So, I worked extremely hard and only spent a month in my aunt's room. I was ready to go down the three steps to my own room.

Before I moved into my original room at Diana's, two of my old roommates from Arcata and my girlfriend at the time helped me get ready to move out of the corner. Together, we worked on fixing up my room. I had to say if I was keeping or letting go of things they had brought from my room in Arcata.

I set aside a ton of stuff to give away. It was hard because I inherited some hoarding tendencies from my mom and grandma, but it's good for the environment to give things away instead of throwing them away.

Once I was home, I thought about how nice it would be to shower alone. When I was in the hospital, having someone shower me was a no-brainer. I couldn't even walk independently for most of that time. At home, it became all I wanted, to stand up with no one helping me. I wanted all the extra people out of my shower time.

The first step to doing that was to phase out Hilda, the caregiver who came to help me during the day when I first came home in February 2020. I urged Diana to cut down

Hilda's hours and ultimately not to have her come to the house anymore.

However, someone had to be with me because I didn't want to use the shower chair anymore, and I wanted to shower standing up. It was still early days in my standing without support.

Instead, Diana started to sit in the bathroom while I lathered, and then she would come into the shower to help me shampoo and rinse out my hair. One day, I told her we should give it a shot with her not coming into the bathroom at all.

A success!

I finally showered from start to finish without anybody helping me, mainly using my left hand. I'm impressed with myself when you consider I was in a near coma not that long before.

There was this patient at CNS I seemed to be always paired up with, sometimes every day of the week. Sometimes, multiple times a day. However, she did not appear to be where I was in the healing process yet. I'm naturally a very empathetic person, maybe too empathetic sometimes.

Whenever I see someone not doing very well, I feel it viscerally; I can't help it. I wanted to connect with her and help her. I'm also naturally a very chatty person, always talking. But she was often negative and would rarely talk to me, no matter what.

Every time we worked together, I was confronted face-to-face with a huge reminder of both how grateful I am that things ended up the way they did, and how things used to be for me and what could have been. Basically, working with her made me uncomfortable and upset, which made it hard for me to concentrate on my recovery. No way was I moving backwards or staying in the same spot when I'd been making so much progress.

I talked to two people about my problems. A cognitive rehab therapist and my case manager. I understood that we had to be paired up occasionally, but I didn't want it to happen as often as it was. I asked whether a third person could be there to talk with me and act as our buffer.

At my request, changes were made in our schedules going forward, and we were not together as often. I could focus much better on the tasks I needed to complete so I could one day not need CNS anymore.

Besides my arm, my right leg is the other part of my body that gave me trouble. I used a leg splint that stretched my contracted muscles. I hated using it and wanted to speed up the process. I wore it every night for a couple of hours while watching TV.

I wanted to increase the tension on it for a long time, but the guy who measured me for it and ordered it said the splint worked best if I wore it for longer periods of time rather than increasing the tension. It didn't improve my ankle's flexibility.

It wasn't working as fast as my physical therapists wanted it to. I don't think he was used to any of his patients asking to up the tension. I kept asking him.

At my request, in October 2020, he finally changed the tension to as high as it would go. He changed it from a four to a seven. Seven is the highest it'll go.

In the new year, I started weaning off the leg splint. I would first wear it for just an hour, then every other day, until I stopped wearing it. I used this wooden triangular stand at CNS to stretch my hamstrings, so we bought one for home. Even though I don't do the exercises any more, I move around as much as I can because that's how I get the rehab to stick.

In December 2020, we started the process to end Diana's conservatorship of my person. It was another huge milestone in my recovery. I had to talk to a lawyer who asked me questions to ensure I was of sound mind. The process was expensive. Unlike Britney Spears, I was kept informed about what was happening at all stages of my conservatorship.[26]

My cognitive and communication skills were back. I could now make my own decisions, and we wanted to open a bank account in my name. However, I still needed a lot of help.

We had documents prepared to give my aunt my power of attorney so she could keep handling my finances, paying my bills, dealing with the insurance company, and other issues. I had too much going on, and I had no desire to take on that work, as it was complicated and overwhelming for me. Diana graciously agreed to continue doing it for as long as I needed.

The bills that come through are so many and so high that they are depressing. I wouldn't have been able to afford the top-of-the-line care I received and the subsequent treatments I tried without inheriting some money from my mom's untimely death.

Having a brain injury, and just living in general, is EXPENSIVE. And keeping track of it all is hard.

I couldn't sign the power of attorney until I was out of the conservatorship. The hearing to end the conservatorship was on July 8, 2021. I had prepared for it with my aunt for

26   Farrow, R., & Tolentino, J. (2021, June 3). Britney Spears's Conservatorship Nightmare. *www.newyorker.com*.

weeks. I talked to my court-appointed lawyer about my recovery and ability to take over.

We didn't need to prepare. I was on the court's video conferencing for maybe 15 minutes. The judge didn't even ask me any questions. Mine was the first case (of many, I'm sure) the judge heard. She opened the court session by saying she had an easy one to give the go-ahead on, so we might as well get it over with first. She granted the termination of my conservatorship!

I learned to advocate for myself. Proactively. When I thought what I was doing in rehab was pointless or seemingly wouldn't help me, I told them, or at least asked how it helped me. I sent a follow-up email when something happened that I was not happy with or confused about. Sometimes with the subject, "SOS."

I'll admit, sometimes I'm impulsive about it. I am quick to complain. Sometimes it was unnecessary, sometimes it got resolved quickly. Sometimes, I send an SOS email before there is even a reason to panic.

It was essential that I speak up because I went so long not being able to advocate for myself. The results spoke for themselves.

getting my voice back
telling people what i need
learning to speak up

chapter 15

before my life changed

why did she hit me
there are 8 billion other
people—wrong place, wrong time

In third grade, my family moved to a big two-story house in Calabasas, California, home of the Kardashians and Kanye West.

My family was always out of place there. We weren't nearly as rich as all the other families, so we didn't have as much help as they did or someone who lived in our house and did everything we asked for. Our house was not as big or fancy as all of theirs.

Later, in my freshman year of high school, my mom, brother, and I moved to a smaller house nearby. My parents had recently divorced. A lot of my life was changing.

I had to adjust to switching between my mom and my dad. That was another reason to add to the list of reasons that we were different. I remember thinking my parents separating right before my bat mitzvah would be the worst thing to happen in my 13-year-old-middle-school self's life.

I went to college as far away as possible from home while still staying in California to pay in-state tuition. I didn't feel like I fit into the San Fernando Valley lifestyle. It was simply somewhere I had lived.

I was part of a family that lived in Calabasas, but it was never home to me. When choosing where to go to college, the only thing to be checked was that it had to be far from Southern California.

I don't remember how I chose Humboldt, other than a friend of my mom's was a professor there in the English department. I was choosing between Humboldt and UC Santa Cruz, but when I got off the waitlist to go to Santa Cruz, they had no on campus housing left.

I was initially an English major because of my connection with Humboldt's English department. I was also interested in pursuing writing as a possible career even then.

Then, we had to attend a meeting during our orientation week for a major other than the one we were already committed to. I chose environmental studies and was so impressed by the curriculum and the head of the department that I ended up switching my major right after starting college.

A few weeks into my sophomore year, my mom called me to tell me her horrible news. I remember she called and told me to sit with the trees while we talked. She knew they would bring me some calm for the news she was about to deliver.

She told me she was sick, with pancreatic cancer, and not to google it because she wouldn't be another statistic. That was one time I did as I was told. I didn't look it up because I genuinely didn't want to know her chances.

Things got progressively worse over that year. She was sick for six months. She told me not to come home and to continue going to school; it was crucial to her. So I stayed at school even though it was next to impossible for me to be so far away. Until that Thanksgiving break and then a few weeks later for winter break.

In the middle of February 2017, I went home for a long weekend that ended up being the beginning of the end for her. I stayed by her side until she passed away in the middle of the night on March 1, 2017.

I went back to school that same week, looking the same but very different inside. And now I had a very cute, teddy bear-looking little dog following me around.

My mom gave me Teddy a few days before she closed her eyes for the last time. I had already cared for him while she was sick, walking and feeding him. So, she asked me to continue doing that when she was gone. I sadly agreed, but it made me feel better to know he would be by my side from then on.

I stayed at my family home with my brothers, Kyle and Teddy, while my mom was hospitalized. The day she died, I took Teddy with me to my aunt's house, where I would live from then on. Then I flew with my new responsibility back to Arcata.

We spent 100% of our time together. I got a letter from my therapist designating him as my emotional support animal before everyone ruined that by trying to certify their peacocks. He went to class with me, to restaurants with me, and on airplanes for free!

He got river days, beach days, and forest days. He loved them all. The day before we were hit by the car was when we celebrated his fifth birthday with his friends, both human and non-human alike. Everyone that loved him had one final night with him. It makes me happy to think about that.

I have around a five-year gap in my memory. Pictures help but looking at pictures can't implant the memory from when that picture was taken into my head. Stories help, too.

I've pieced together most of my life through stories. Who I lost my virginity to, how old I was when I smoked weed and drank for the first time, and the bands I've seen live. Because I had to hear this through stories, I feel extremely disassociated from pre-accident Emily.

When I hear stories about myself from people who knew the old version of Em, they usually sound like what I would do, but I can't imagine doing most of it. I have no or very vague memories left of many things. I really enjoy hearing stories of my life.

Because I have no memory associated with them, it's almost like I'm hearing a story about someone else. Not me. It's the weirdest feeling. I don't think there is a word to describe it. Disassociation comes close.

It's like you're hearing a story about someone else, and then you find out it was really you the whole time. That's the best way I can describe it.

My brain is bizarre with what it chooses to latch onto. Like, I do remember the food Teddy ate. Salmon and sweet potato kibble in a blue and orange bag. I also remember every single one of my elementary school teachers' names.

I don't really remember when my mom was sick or when she died. I also don't remember ever having sex with anybody. I remember everyone I've been intimate with and the extent of our relationship. I just don't remember the actual act itself.

In high school, I was on the swim team and played water polo for two and a half years. However, I have absolutely no memory associated with this; but I remember loving being in the water. We luckily have a pool in our backyard, and I first went in it in late April of 2020.

The first few times we went into the pool, I mostly sat in my pool floatie. Kicking against the water. Then I turned it into a workout for me. I worked on walking against the resistance of the water.

Swimming was always a big thing for me, but now it highlighted how my body wasn't really working yet. I could kick, hold my breath, and do what looked enough like swimming with my right arm. Things changed when I bought a pair of goggles. They changed everything.

At first, I swam with an inflatable strapped around my waist. I wasn't allowed to go in the deep end for a while. I could only swim a short distance, and someone always had to be in the pool with me. Diana was worried I'd drown.

On the other hand, I was itching to jump in the pool and swim in the deep end. I figured I've been swimming my whole life, and if a freaking car hitting me doesn't kill me, then jumping in the pool can't. Eventually, she said I could jump into the pool.

It was anticlimactic.

I just cannonballed into the deep end, and that was that.

Sometimes I wonder if my accident had happened to any other person, would they have healed as well as me? It was an accident, although I don't understand how you can genuinely not see a whole person and a dog crossing a freaking crosswalk. So, it could have happened to anyone.

Really the perfect example of being in the wrong place at the wrong time. It wouldn't have happened if one of us had left two minutes earlier or later. If it had happened to someone else, they might not have fought so hard for their life to be livable again. I did.

life is sometimes hard
i wonder who makes the choice
can there be a god?

chapter 16

love your brain

I am most myself
when I am writing a poem
not a thing matters

Before my brain injury, I didn't take good care of my brain. I smoked pot multiple times a day, every day.

I had occasionally also tried other types of drugs like mushrooms and ecstasy. I was experimenting, not thinking about any repercussions. It was college.

The neurologist in the ICU in Eureka asked my aunt what kinds of drugs I had done in the past. All Diana knew was that I smoked weed because I had gotten in trouble my senior year of high school for smoking pot in my car.

I had just left to go to McDonald's and thought I would get my mom and me ice cream cones. Then, when I gave it to her, I guess I smelled like weed.

My mom went out to my car, which I had just been smoking in so it reeked of weed. She found out. All because

I was trying to be nice. While I was high. Which wasn't the best idea.

After she punished me, my mom called two of her friends to tell them what her daughter was doing. One of those friends was Diana.

Diana had to ask my friends to fill in the blanks in order to answer the neurologist's question. I, of course, didn't know this was happening, and I am very happy they told her everything. I admit I was sort of hurt, though, that they did tell her everything, but mostly, I am proud of them for telling her.

One time, early during my recovery period, the nurses at Northridge asked me what I did for fun. I didn't have a filter at that point. I didn't know there were certain things you shouldn't just blurt out.

So, I responded with, "I like to do drugs."

I'm not sure why I said that instead of saying reading, writing, or taking walks. Admittedly, I felt cooped up, sick of the hospital, and missed the easy days when I smoked pot. I just said what was on my mind.

I smoked weed again for the first time since my accident almost two years later, on May 14, 2021. I sat around a bonfire late at night in the dark and made s'mores with one of my best friends. My first smoking buddy.

We each smoked a small joint filled with a 75 percent smoking mix filled with peppermint, clove, and mugwort. I had been planning it for a while and talked to my neurologist about it in March 2021 to ensure my safety.

The neurologist warned me that it might cause a different reaction in my brain than it had before. I had gone to the dentist and had a cavity filled a few months earlier. When they gave me Novocain (or something like it), my heart started beating so fast, and my hands began to shake. That made me nervous that my brain might react badly when introduced again to weed for the first time in a long time.

I visited the dispensary the week before I smoked to prepare. I told them I used to smoke multiple times a day but stopped because I was hit by a car nineteen months before. They gave me an eighth of this CBD-dominant 1:1 strain called Doctor's Orders.

Turns out, I had no reason to be nervous! I didn't really get anxious or stressed. I just had thoughts flying through my brain a million miles a minute. I became super hungry and relished eating my s'more.

My friend joined me and brought cheesecake, which we dug into after the fire. Then, after she left, I washed my face and brushed my teeth. I went to sleep easily and slept for eleven hours.

Joint-rolling is a skill I thought I didn't have anymore. I thought the joint I was about to roll wouldn't even look close to what it should be. The first time, it took me a little longer than it used to, but muscle memory kicked in.

I think rolling up an herb should be regularly included in rehab programs. It takes hand-eye coordination and focus. Doing it was much slower than the last time I smoked weed almost two years prior, but it was still beautifully rolled. Muscle memory, I guess.

Since that first time, I began smoking once a week. I usually just watched a funny movie while I was high and went to sleep very easily and soundly. I luckily don't struggle to sleep. I sleep for a long time and sleep like a rock.

The title of this chapter came from an organization headquartered in Los Angeles that was started by a guy who suffered a traumatic brain injury while training for the 2010 Winter Olympics. One of my family friends bought me a t-shirt from them. So I looked them up and was inspired to name this chapter after the organization.

They hold yoga retreats for people with TBIs. They also teach others how to teach yoga to people with TBIs. One of my physical therapists was trained to teach it. We did their special kind of yoga a few times.

Brain injuries, like everything in life, fall on a spectrum. I was a fairly high functioning brain-injured person at the brain injury rehab clinic. As such, I saw the whole spectrum of patients. I understood and was happy that I exemplified the higher end of the spectrum, something for other patients to aspire to.

I unfortunately also saw the other end. People carried a piece of paper reminding them of who they were, where they were, and why they were there. Other people worked in physical therapy just to roll from one side to the other.

I was learning to live with a traumatic brain injury, and I felt like there was very little that I had control over. I started obsessing over certain things; specifically, what I was going to eat on a weekly basis.

Back in the hospital, I had to choose my three meals for the next day. I think my need for control over my eating came from this habit during my time in the hospital. For many months, I also decided over the weekend what to eat for breakfast that week. Then came lunch, depending on what I would have for breakfast. They had to go well together. Or I would have brunch once I got home if I got to sleep in late enough.

After I was home at Diana's, I would make a list and give it to my aunt so she could do the shopping and cooking for the week. A big reason I was like that is because I felt like I lacked control in my life. This was a small way to take some of it back.

I also chose everything I would wear for the week before it began. I laid my clothes out on a chair in my room, waiting for me to be ready. I would lay them out on Monday, Tuesday, Wednesday, Thursday, and Friday on the arm of the chair. The weekend outfits had to go on the chair seat because there wasn't enough room on the arms. Control over at least some aspects of my life.

Some days, I would cry in physical therapy. Not because the exercises were too hard for me. Or because they hurt me. I just would get very overwhelmed.

I understand I have a brain injury, an affliction that will stay with me for the rest of my life. It's not like a broken leg that will heal eventually. No one knows how much healing I will get through rehab. I am writing this in Fall 2021, and hope that it will be better than it is right now.

The reality is I was hit by a car. Nothing anyone does can change that. It's just about getting as better as my body and mind can. I have no idea what that'll look like.

I stayed hopeful that if I kept going to rehab and doing everything I was supposed to, that my future would be better. I couldn't get worse from there on out. I was already in a near-coma once.

writing my story
don't know how it will end up
i just have to write

chapter 17

i can see clearly now[27]

here i am living
but not really working right
when i could be dead

My life has become immeasurably different since the accident. Everything I knew, everything I was, everything I wanted to be. It all changed in an instant. I don't want it to be, but it is.

My body is only about 80%, 85% at best. I can't remember a huge portion of my life. Defining moments that are just gone to me. I have become a new version of myself since the accident. Not always a better me. A more impatient, intolerant person, but also a more empathetic and understanding person. My whole life has been separated into before the accident and after the accident.

27   Legaspi, A. (2020, October 7). Johnny Nash, ‘ I can See Clearly Now’ singer, dead at 80. Rolling Stone. https://www.rollingstone.com/music/music-news/johnny-nash-obituary-1071981/

There's old Emily and now Emily. Both pretty funny and smart, but physically and mentally very different. Everything seems different now.

Working on standing, walking, and strengthening my body took center stage in my life and in rehab sessions. But I also needed to work on my vision. My eyes didn't focus on the same thing at once. One pupil moves slightly above the other.

I've had glasses since I was 14. I've always had astigmatism and started wearing glasses after middle school. Mostly because I thought they looked cute on me. Getting hit by a car made my vision much worse. My glasses weren't just to look cute anymore.

Back when I first started with CNS, I told my therapists during my first week there that I couldn't do a reading assessment because I didn't have my glasses. I knew I had glasses but wasn't sure why I wore them. I couldn't see far away, though.

Post-accident me has little to no depth perception. I took in my glasses the next day, but they didn't help anymore.

I went to an optometrist who specializes in brain injuries for the first time in June 2020. I went twice and he did a ton of tests on me. He discovered my eyes did not work well together. I finally got my new pair of glasses on July 10, 2020, which were adjusted a few months later.

Ironically, now I desperately need glasses. With them I have 20/20 vision in one eye and 25/20 in the other. They also have prisms in them to help realign my eyes.

With them, I can read even the tiny subtitles on the TV. Before, I was walking up to the TV whenever there were subtitles. It's crazy to think that I was seeing everything so blurry before.

The doctor also prescribed light therapy as part of my CNS occupational therapy. That is when I spend ten minutes staring at a lamp in these blue-green lensed glasses and ten minutes staring at it wearing red-orange lenses.

One of them was supposed to help my balance. The other was for the motion sickness I got in cars. I think, more than anything, the glasses helped me not get carsick anymore.

According to him, this therapy helps improve concentration, sleep, energy, and visual awareness. Light therapy also supposedly helps improve balance, makes reading easier, helps people retain information better, improves attitude, and makes coordination better than it was before.

Towards the end of September 2020, my neuro-optometrist said I didn't have to do the light therapy for at least two months. He then reinstated me on light therapy for just four weeks in February of 2021, except just with one pair of the two lenses he initially gave me.

Instead of twice for ten minutes, it was for twenty whole minutes. Since I was doing it at home, I listened to music for twenty minutes to make the time slightly more bearable.

For a second opinion, I tried the second of the two neuro-optometrists that the clinic works with. He was twice the distance from the first doctor, but the traveling was worth it to have another doctor look at my eyes.

Since my goal was to drive again, my vision had to be the best it could be. We did two and a half hours of testing, and that was just the first of two assessments to see how my vision was.

He had me draw a clock, something I had been doing since I could first hold a pencil at the clinic. It helps them figure out how I handled spatial relationships. Then, he had me mark the center of various lines. Another thing I've done a bunch of times before. He had me stand with my feet together and my arms crossed to observe my balance.

He also had me do things I'd never done before.

He checked my peripheral vision with a little glowing light coming into my sideline of vision, and I would press this little button. He noted that my right eye was much worse than my left, something I already knew.

The left eye can only overcompensate so much. He told me that I have a limited line of sight towards the right side of me. He said that was gone forever. My line of sight is forever damaged.

Then, four weeks after my initial assessment, I returned to that eye doctor for the second of the two evaluations. He had me walk in squares repeatedly so he could see my turning radius.

On this cool machine, I showed him my side-vision abilities (they are really lacking). There, they had me reading paragraphs to examine how my eyes scanned the page. They also looked at my eyeballs up close on another machine.

In June 2021, my new neuro-optometrist prescribed me light therapy again. I was initially pissed because I hated light therapy as it was very boring. However, it was only for two sets of thirty seconds each and used new lenses. They were very different from the other lenses I used and were a stimulant.

These looked orange, while the other ones were blue and green. My new neuro-optometrist wanted the new orange lenses to wake something up in my brain that's been turned off because of my accident.

I'm afraid to think about the future. To be too hopeful. I know what I would like to happen in an ideal world, but in an ideal world, I never would have been hit by a car. So, I try to resist being too hopeful about the coming months.

What if it doesn't happen that way?

I do know that I've shattered other expectations. I mean, one of the first neurologists who saw me at Barlow told my dad that it could be a freakin' year before I would be able to talk.

Another doctor at Northridge told my aunt that my right arm might never straighten out, because it had been so long already. At least I'm not silently existing with a contracted arm, bent at the elbow up to my shoulder.

"You're so much better."

I hear this a lot.

I know that I am getting better, and I don't need everyone to remind me of how far I've come. I remember what it was like.

Whether I like it or not, my body remembers what it was like. I don't always appreciate it when people tell me how much better things are now than they used to be.

I mean, I like knowing that now is better than life was for me a year before, but I don't like when the past is so bluntly pointed out. The past is in the past for a reason.

We've moved *past* the past. It's in our so-called rearview mirrors for a reason.

That's a whole other thing. What's the reason for anything in our past? What was the reason for me getting hit by a car? Was there a reason? Is there ever going to be a reason? Or do things just happen sometimes, for no reason?

i'm a new person
polka dots on my fingers
grounding me in time

chapter 18

problems i've had since my life was changed

i was very hurt
then i got broken up with
life just sucks sometimes

About six months after my accident, to add insult to injury, my then girlfriend—I'll just call her my ex—broke up with me. We just weren't meant to be together. She was amazing to me while I was in the various hospitals and first recovering at home, so I was sad but not surprised because she had done this same thing approximately a week before my accident.

We had a toxic relationship. Always breaking up and then making up, usually within days. As I became more cognitively aware, read my old journals, and remembered more, I realized how unhealthy and back-and-forth it was, and how long it had been that way.

It just comes down to this: She was scared of our relationship and wasn't ready for what it could be. Like most of the girls I've been with.

I think part of it is because I'm an Aries, and we love hard and fast. She was the only girl, actually, to have a break-up talk with me. All the other ones have just faded away.

We weren't meant to be together as a couple. We had very different priorities and paths in life. For some reason, our paths crossed for a few years. I struggle to find that reason.

We never had an anniversary, and when I asked why we didn't, that led to the break-up. We never actually became a couple, we just started regularly holding hands randomly. We started off as roommates before becoming neighbors. Then, we became whatever we were.

She was never officially my girlfriend. My ex would say she fell into it because everyone thought of her as that. We both just got caught up in it. I was very excited because I'd already wanted it for a few years.

She had never even come close to being with a girl before me. She started off my interest by flirting with me. I would've been totally fine just being her friend.

My ex asked me in 2021 if I would have preferred her just being my friend when I woke up from my near coma. I said yes, but I think she was officially my girlfriend at the time. I needed someone to dote on me. We basically were a couple without the title.

At my first hospital, a doctor wanted to give someone information about me. Everyone looked at her because she said she was my girlfriend. She wasn't really, and there wasn't a word to accurately portray our relationship to one another, but that was enough for right then.

My ex fell into the role of my girlfriend after that. Mostly because she thought I would need a person to be close to throughout my recovery. In retrospect, I did need her like that at that point, but it did make it harder when she pulled out of my life.

At first, she was just my former roommate who liked to eat the food I made. I would constantly go over to her place down the street and make us dinner to share. I like to cook, and she liked to eat what I cooked.

I'm prone to helping girls discover their most authentic identities. After many years of therapy, I think it gives me this weird satisfaction. She wasn't the first "straight" girl to fall for me. So, maybe I like them questioning because I never have to try very hard to get them to consider ladies more closely.

Most women I've been with were not interested in women before me. Like her, they always considered it but never followed through on that thought. Until me. This is both a positive and a negative. Mostly a negative.

She was the best one of my exes to be with me during my accident. If she was anything, she was reliable. She was by my side like it was her job. She moved from Arcata to Los Angeles when I was flown down here.

She told me there was no way she'd stay in that tiny town without me. Just getting updates every so often. She said that would've been unbearable. Instead, she was the one giving people updates several times a week.

Basically, every day, she would drive to wherever I was and spend time with me. She went to every hospital I was placed in and wore a visitor's pass when needed. She took multiple shifts a week when I was at Barlow, Texhoma, and even spent nights with me at Northridge. She would often fill in when no one else could come.

She wasn't allowed to sleep in my bed with me at Northridge hospital when she stayed the night with me during my stay there. The beds were rigged with an alarm system that would go off if there was more than one person in the bed after a certain time. So, they made her sleep on a cot that they would wheel in whenever she slept over.

We would push the cot very close to my bed, so it was almost like we were sleeping together. My ex was in my life 200% at that time and met almost everyone that worked with me. She would lie down beside me in the hospital bed to watch movies with me.

For some reason, the last hospital I was in had the best movies. Even very new and recent movies. So we had a great selection to choose from.

At that point, it was impossible for me to make a definitive choice about most things. So, she would usually make the executive decision for us. We were given so many choices, that sometimes we would choose two movies. Either watch them back-to-back in one sitting if she was staying all night, or save the other one for the next time she was there. She would come often during my three-week stay.

My ex continued to visit me once I was home. She didn't visit for a while after the breakup because of the pandemic and because we both needed a break. I was left with these weird feelings.

I know the breakup was the best thing for me. In a theoretical world, I would've broken up with her if she hadn't broken up with me and I had never been hit by a car.

She stopped coming in July 2020. We kept fighting whenever we talked. She chose to block me on every form of communication.

I know it was very messy and hurtful when we would talk. It upset me when we wouldn't communicate when she spent almost a year supporting me, seeing me daily, and being by my side.

By late February 2021, we weren't talking at all. This might not have been the worst thing, but it left me feeling abandoned and like I lost another best friend after my accident. I know she's not dead, but she may as well have been.

She and I just have a weird but pure love for each other. Not exactly in the way I've wanted, but I've come to know that it's what I needed.

I did need her to be my girlfriend during my hospitalization. I needed someone there to kiss and physically hold me. It was still very confusing for me though, as it was before I got injured.

We went from zero to 60 in like 10 seconds. Having a relationship during the hardest parts of my recovery would have been messy anyway. I needed to focus on myself, not a girlfriend, for a few years.

The plan was that once I healed and knew what I wanted from this life, I would be back in the dating pool. My dating options were limited because rehab wasn't the best place to meet cuties. Quite honestly, it would mean losing my virginity all over again.

I started trying to get comfortable with just seeing her as my friend. That's what we were for much longer than we were together. It's not the time for us to be friends yet, though. Everything is still too raw.

I honestly don't remember most of our relationship. I do remember the constant breakups—at least once a month.

I didn't want to be broken up with, though. She would say, "Maybe we should go back to being friends?" and I would respond with, "I don't think it's time for us." She was a pushover, and I was, and still am, pushy. Pretty hard-headed and stubborn.

When I got hurt, my ex began living for me, not herself. That was when she broke up with me. When she realized she wasn't living life for herself anymore.

I know we're not supposed to be a couple. I'm not even sure we're supposed to be friends. At least not right now. I asked her for space, but I didn't think it would go from her moving nine hours south to be near me, to not talking to each other for months.

I think that most people come into your life for a reason. I thought I knew what our reason was, but I guess I don't yet.

It would be even harder if I remembered all the parts of our relationship. My ex remembers everything that had happened between us over the years. She answered my questions when I asked them.

I really thought about my questions before I asked them to ensure I phrased them correctly. I asked her probably too many questions, but I think if you make your bed, you should sleep in it.

I asked about our first kiss, and how we knew we were more than friends. I firmly believe those are memories I will never get back. My brain is just too broken to hold onto them any longer. If they come back to me, and it's a huge if, I'll be pleasantly surprised.

I think I'm happy that she still has those memories. It's a good thing that they still exist in one of us. It also is probably good that they're not in me.

I've always known that my feelings went deeper than hers. I always knew that we didn't love each other the same amount. Or in the same way. That's why I wasn't surprised when she broke up with me.

Most of our relationship was me trying to convince her that she was worthy of my love. You can't convince another person of a lesson like that. There was nothing I could say or do to tell her that she was worthy of my love.

She had to come to that conclusion herself. Not just my love but anybody's. You know that age-old saying, *you can't love someone else until you love yourself.*

It's tough to be the one in a relationship who wants it to go on. I accepted that we were not supposed to be together romantically at the time, but I unconsciously added *at the time* and now it's a problem. I honestly don't think we'll ever be together again mostly because I know that she doesn't want it. That's the thing I'm struggling with.

Through all this, why would I want to be with someone who doesn't want to be with me? I think it's because it would weirdly make me feel worthier. If I convinced her. I don't want to have to convince someone to want to be with me.

Maybe it's something from my childhood that makes me think that way. I have no idea where it comes from. I know it's not the right way to be thinking.

Every story has two sides, and I realize hers isn't the same as mine. I knew she felt our future was best with us just as friends. I was struggling to catch up. I agreed that we didn't work that great as a couple, and while I was recovering it wasn't the time for me to be in a relationship with anyone. I needed to focus on myself.

Who knows what would have happened between us had I never been hit by a car? I was graduating from college, and we were headed in very different directions.

I probably would have eventually broken up with her had I stayed up there. Either way, it would've been very hard and messy. Probably just as messy as it was when it happened, if not messier.

She broke up with me because I saw a future that she didn't. Or couldn't. Maybe even a future that she didn't want to see.

She broke up with me through a FaceTime call. Maybe all the other times wouldn't stick because she could see my face in person. It was easier to not be with me when it happened. For her, for sure, but maybe also for me. Since we were in the middle of a pandemic and she lived two hours away, we hadn't been seeing each other in person except on special occasions.

I don't know if she woke up that morning intending to leave me. I know she'd been thinking of it since even before I was injured; I guess I just said something that was the straw that broke the camel's back.

She's gone back to the town where I was hurt multiple times. I know I don't have any ownership over that town because I was injured there. I thought and probably will always think that because my life irrevocably changed there, I should have been consulted before a visit.

The first time was a few weeks after she promised we'd go together and said she'd never return without me. The second was during a fight of ours.

I was furious that she'd returned there without even giving me a heads-up. I'm not sure why her going there hurt me so much. Maybe it was because I couldn't go back by myself yet. Maybe it was because she ignored the promise she'd made me.

Or maybe it was that the place meant so many heavy things for me that the thought of someone else having a relationship with that town was offensive. We were in the middle of a fight anyway. To top it off, I found out she was back there through social media. Not even a text or a call.

She broke my heart. Shattered it into a million pieces. At a time when I really didn't know what was happening. We certainly didn't have the healthiest relationship. We were constantly breaking up and getting back together. I didn't remember any of that when I woke up from my coma, near coma, or whatever it was.

My memory was so bad, I mistakenly thought she had taken my virginity! I didn't remember our fights or our inability to be on the same page.

Reflecting on us as a pair, in 2021, when I put the finishing touches on this chapter, I realized how blind I was to the realitics of our relationship just before my accident. We had broken up days before I was hit, but she was by my side through all the hospitals.

I had forgotten that we'd broken up when I came to. For whatever reason, she had moved to be near me, never reminding me of the breakup.

She told one of my earliest doctors she was my girlfriend because she wanted medical information. When I woke up, though, I knew her as my very present girlfriend who had moved 9+ hours south to be near me.

I didn't remember the fights. She didn't remind me.

She would kiss my face and even sleep in my hospital rooms. I didn't know the realities of our relationship until after she had broken up with me. My therapist, who I've been seeing since before the accident, reminds me of the realities of our situation. Both past and present.

It was very overwhelming for me to deal with so much at once.

I had to handle my dog dying, not dreaming at night, my right arm not working correctly, not walking perfectly, and my girlfriend breaking up with me. It's too much for one person to take on. Even just one of those things would be a lot, but all of them?

I want to sleep until everything is better, for a few weeks or even years. I know that's impossible though. I get overwhelmed as a result. That probably isn't the best thing for my recovery, but it is what it is.

I'm working on acceptance. Learning to understand that there are so many things I want to change so badly, but I simply can't.

having to heal my
mind, body, and heart at once
it is all too much

chapter 19

the prosecution

i was just walking
when i was struck by a car
now this is my life

People have told me that I had been having a good day on the day of our accident. I went to Los Bagels that morning with my roommate, Zoe. Los Bagels is a small bagel shop in Arcata.

I probably ordered a toasted garlic bagel with cream cheese, a special Humboldt sweet mustard sauce, red onions, and microgreens. That was my usual order. Maybe I had lox if I was feeling splurgy.

We probably got home around noon. The car made contact with my body sometime close to 5:30. Those five hours in between are a total mystery. The driver stole that day and many more from me.

Since finding out what had happened to us, I've gone through every emotion you can think of toward the woman who hit me. Anger turned into hate, and it permeated every-thing, especially in the beginning.

The driver was arrested and the complaint charged her with "the crime of Driving Under The Influence Of An Alcoholic Beverage Causing Injury in violation of VC23153(a), a Felony."

This is the letter I wrote to the judge who would preside over the driver's case when she would eventually be prosecuted for her crime against me.

April 15, 2020

To the Honorable Judge,

I am writing about the driver who hit me on September 7, 2019. How dare she hit me? Why would she drive drunk? She killed my dog and he was the best dog ever. I am very mad at her, and I hate her!!! I really wish that she had taken a different road that day that did not have us on it. I wish she had not driven drunk and made the horrible decision to drive drunk that day. I hope she gets punished for this. Because of what she did, my life has been impacted in so many ways.

Because she almost killed me. I am in this condition because of her. I was in a near coma because of her. I can't walk on my own because of her. I can't use my right hand because of her! She does not really know how she has affected me. She took many of my memories. I can't dream at night. She ruined my life for now but I am working hard to get it back.

I was loved before this by a lot of people but this gave them the opportunity to really show me how much. I am very loved and doubt that she is. I hope she goes to jail for longer than it takes me to get better. Please do not let her go free.

Emily Owen

In re-reading the letter to the judge, I can now see how different I was then. I had to dictate the letter. My sentences and vocabulary were simple.

My reasoning was very basic and visceral. Sometimes almost childish. I realize how different I was early in my recovery and how far I have come.

By June 2020, my thinking about the driver had started to change. First, I emailed the Assistant District Attorney on my case, thanking him for fighting for me. This caused him to set up a phone call with me.

He told me that as a victim of a crime in California, I was constitutionally entitled to have a speedy trial. It had already been nine months since my accident, so it didn't seem very speedy of them.

The pandemic had slowed everything down and her lawyer kept calling for continuances, so things got pushed off even further. You'd think only a few months would go by after a crime like the one done to me.

Because of the coronavirus, everything had been messed up. The driver continued walking around free, not changed by her horrible decision.

Unfortunately, I could barely even walk at that point because of her decisions, when she chose to drive after drinking and then to look in her center console at the exact moment we were crossing in the CROSSWALK. I admittedly have also been so stupid as to drive after drinking a beer but, thankfully, I have never hurt anyone.

She did severely hurt me though. For the rest of my life, I will now be working through the pain she caused me, both emotionally and physically. She made the terrible decision to do something that unfortunately ruined the life I was living and changed me forever.

I think about the converse side and how much worse things could have been for me. I mean, I come face to face with the theoretical converse side every day at rehab. I guess she stood in the way of me living a carefree life.

She unexpectedly sent me down a new, different path in life. I wouldn't ever say it was a better path. Just different. However, I will never forgive her.

I know forgiveness is good for your soul, but I also know some actions are unforgivable. Not only did she leave me with irreparable emotional, physical, and cognitive deficits that I might forever need to work through, she also killed my best friend, my constant companion, the living reminder of my mom.

That woman's actions led to him losing his life while still young. I can never forgive that woman for his sake or for the version of me that was killed along with him. I can never and will never forget what happened.

A preliminary hearing was scheduled for the middle of July 2020. Another continuance was a possibility. Almost a whole freaking year after she hit us. The DA explained the process to me. He told me that opposing the continuance would mean more coming from me, the victim of a crime, than from his office.

I was dreading having to see her on the computer when I delivered the message. So I asked Diana to tell the DA that I couldn't miss rehab, and he said that was the perfect reason to miss the hearing. He said he would oppose a continuance on my behalf.

For months, I wanted the driver to suffer. I wanted her to burn. I wished the worst for her. Things I'm a little ashamed of for even coming up with. Then, one day in June, I told my therapist at CNS, "Ya know, I think I would prefer her to do multiple years worth of community service instead of going to jail."

This was at the peak of the coronavirus, and fewer trials were taking place and I think they were even releasing inmates to reduce crowding in the jails. So who knows what would come out of a trial.

I don't think she'll ever hit another person, or dog, with a car. I don't think she set out that Saturday afternoon to severely injure someone and kill a dog.

To top it all off, the driver is a single mom with four kids. Who would watch them if she went to jail? I know what it's like to not have a mother present, and it sucks. I wouldn't do that to them.

I told the DA on my case that I didn't want the driver to go to jail. He didn't seem to think avoiding jail was the best idea. As I remember it, he said the crime she committed by driving drunk was a crime against the community, not just me. I was insistent.

Eventually, he agreed to support my decision and defer to me. Many sometimes forget the victims in the process, but he didn't. He told me that if I was sure, then he would make it a priority for her to complete hundreds of hours of community service instead.

I mean, she has to live with that guilt weighing on her every single day for the rest of her life. She has to go to sleep at night with the image of hitting me with her car playing over and over in her mind. Since she killed Teddy and seriously injured me, I wanted her to actively work to make that community better as a punishment.

I also told the DA that I wanted her to read everyone's impact letter. People like Diana, my dad, every roommate I've had, my ex-girlfriend, and many friends all wrote letters to the judge about the impact her drunk driving had on me. I also said that while I wouldn't talk to her, she could write me a letter and I would read it.

Instead of having a preliminary hearing, the DA talked to her defense attorney and offered that she complete 400 hours of community service instead of having a jury trial. He told them that the offer came directly from me. I think that neither she nor her defense attorney wanted a jury trial anyway.

I was told she wanted to talk to me and apologize for her huge mistake. I said I was not comfortable hearing her voice. I didn't want to talk to her; instead, she could talk to my aunt and dad.

At my request, Diana promised me that she wouldn't accept an apology on my behalf from the driver. An apology would never make me walk correctly, fix my right hand, fix my brain, or bring my dog back to life. It would only serve to make her feel better.

I'm sure she already knew that her actions had consequences, but I wanted her to feel it. Experience it, unfortunately not as close as me, but as close as possible after the fact.

On the morning of August 26 2020, almost a year after the accident, while I was at rehab, Diana had a phone call with the lady who hit me. The driver wanted to apologize.

My aunt told me that most of the time she stayed quiet, just listening to the woman. I told Diana I wanted the driver to know everything I went through at the hospitals and rehab, so Diana told her about it all.

It was sickening for me to hear about their conversation. It humanized the driver. Hating her when she was a nameless demon to me was a lot easier. For 11 months, she was to me just the crazy lady who hit me with her car.

Then, suddenly, that changed. Now, she was just a human being that made a terrible decision. One that Teddy and I had to pay the price for.

I'm sure she's also living in her own hell. She told Diana that she was a Dianic Wiccan, which I looked up and means worshiping female goddesses and believing in the power of the female. She said she was praying and lighting candles for me all the time.

The driver also said she was going to work to get the place where I was hit turned into a four-way stop. So something like this would never happen to anyone else again. She cried on the phone and told my aunt she thought of me daily.

At first, I told Diana that I had only one question for her to ask on my behalf. Did Teddy and I dent the woman's car when she hit us? My aunt said she would ask if I really wanted her to. After some thinking, I decided that more information wouldn't change anything that happened. I didn't need the answer to my question.

Usually, I would have asked those questions. I have a ton of questions that will probably never be answered. What kind of car had she been driving? Part of me even wanted to know what color the car was. I'm okay if these questions never get answered.

They won't keep me up at night or bring me any kind of closure. I mean, I was hit by a car. My dog was killed in our accident. It never should have happened, but it did. Closure is something we made up to feel better. It isn't real.

There is no way to go back in time and change that. My life was flipped upside down. So was hers. The driver has to live with this for the rest of her life. I think she's only in her thirties, so that's a long time to have this hanging over her head.

She destroyed both of our lives with her reckless choice. Mine for a few years, hopefully, and hers forever.

My dad also talked to the driver on the phone. At the time, I didn't want to hear about what they talked about. It was intense enough for me to listen to Diana's conversation with her.

Months later, he gave me a short play-by-play of their conversation. Apparently, a detective had told her I was brain-dead, so she didn't find out what really happened to me for almost a year.

Not wanting the driver to go to prison showed my brain healing on more complex levels. Not entirely yet, but more than it had in a long time. I never believed in jail doing what it is supposed to do, and I still don't.

I don't think she's a terrible person. I just think that she made a really, really terrible decision that day. I don't think she'd ever do something like this again, but she significantly endangered me and our entire community.

So, jail wouldn't stick it to her—community service might. At the very least, it might protect other people from having this happen to them. She could talk to people or maybe even help people who did get injured.

I ideally wanted the driver to work to clean the forest in Arcata. She would pick up trash and be thinking about

THE BEST OF THE WORST

what had happened. The forest was Teddy's favorite place we would go, so it seemed fitting.

September 3, 2020 is the day the driver pled guilty. She took the plea bargain in court almost a year after she hit me. 361 days later. It was also the day I read the letter I said she could write to me.

The letter she sent me was the most BS thing I've ever read.

She apologized and wrote that she lit prayer candles in my honor daily. The driver sent me condolences for the death of Teddy and said that she loved dogs. She said she had adopted multiple dogs and worked at an animal shelter. She said how incredibly sorry she was a few times. She also praised me for my capacity for mercy.

Reading the letter didn't make me feel anything at the time, but knowing she knew Teddy's name made me sick. Nothing she could say could make what happened right. Still, I feel like reading it was a massive step in my healing process. Especially because it didn't create any feelings in me, good or bad; reading it was just something I did, like getting hit by a car is just something that happened to me.

Nothing anyone says or does will make that right. Now, it's just about minimizing hurt.

On the year anniversary of my accident, I wrote a response to the driver's letter. I couldn't let her have the final word. Here's my letter to her:

Sept 7, 2020
Dear Driver,

I'm writing in response to your letter. I didn't think you should get the last word on this, because you hit me with a car and killed my dog, you don't deserve that.

Reading it was medium. Nothing you could ever say to me would make this right. It also didn't really make me feel worse necessarily. Well, it did kind of make me feel worse because it humanized you.

You were a heck of a lot easier to hate when you were just a demon. I think it's great that you and your friends light candles for me, but honestly, those candles aren't helping me. My hard work and determination are.

I spent months in a hospital because of your mistake. I'm sure it was hard for you to be the person who hit someone else with a car and live with that guilt every day, but it has been horrible to be me for the last year.

You sending me your condolences for losing Teddy made me feel heartbroken all over again. I get that you work at animal shelters, but you took the greatest dog away from me, so I hope you think about him every time you even see a dog.

I don't know if I'll ever be 100% again. My personality, thank God, is back 100%, but I cannot walk normally. My right arm can't straighten totally. I don't dream at night, I haven't for a year. I'm not sure if I ever will again.

I have about a five-year memory gap. I don't remember graduating college, losing my virginity, or my mother dying. I'm working very hard every single day to reclaim my life from your horrible decision. I don't know what my life will look like in the future, but then again I didn't know 364 days ago that you were going to hit me with a car. But, oh well, it is what it is.

I know you have a lot of kids, and I didn't want to leave them without a mom. They weren't in the car with you when you hit me. How would you feel if one of them was hit by a car? Just when they were innocently walking their dog. I, unfortunately, have to deal with that and a dead best friend.

Now, I'm working with what I've got, and I've worked hard to accept that it's not what most 23-year-olds are dealing with. But it is what I'm dealing with for some reason.

Emily

On October 26, 2020, the driver had her sentencing hearing. Diana helped me send in my statement to the probation officer. This was it:

My name is Emily Owen, and I was hit by the car the defendant was driving while under the influence on September 7, 2019.

Her actions have devastated my life. However, through the Assistant District Attorney I have previously expressed my wish that the defendant serve community service instead of going to jail. I agree with the guilty plea of the felony of driving under the influence causing bodily harm and that probation be granted instead of jail time.

It is important to me that the community service be served over at least two years, with no early termination.

I was an Environmental Studies major. My dog died as a result of the defendant's actions on September 7, 2019. My dog and I loved going to the beach and hiking in the

forest. There is a beach/forest clean-up program that would be my program of choice for her community service. See http://pacoutgreenteam.org/. I implore you to make this happen.

Many of my friends and family wrote letters to the judge that were sent to the DA's office. It is my wish that the defendant read all of these letters in the presence of either her attorney or the Probation Officer.

Sincerely,

Emily Owen

October 15, 2020

The sentencing hearing was held over Zoom, and a few of my friends, my dad, and Diana watched it. I went to rehab. The driver apologized once again.

Instead of jail time, she got 400 hours of community service. She was put on probation for five years (which I believe includes reporting to a probation officer), needs a breathalyzer on her car for two years, and I was told her license would be revoked for a time, but I don't know for how long.

I don't feel as good as I thought I would feel once this chapter was kind of closed. I guess that's because physically my body still isn't working as it's supposed to, and I don't know if it will ever.

I still have cognitive and mental deficits. That won't go away, unfortunately, when she at least knows what her near-future will be like. I definitely won't be the same person I once was again.

That person didn't know how good she had it. Or even how lucky she was to dream at night. Or how very blessed and lucky she was every time she took her dog on a walk. I didn't take things lightly in the past, but I took things for granted. I had no idea how lucky I was to live that care-free life.

i feel like this is
the way it's supposed to be
sucks that i got hit

chapter 20

the final stretch

*i was injured but
i am a dandelion,
growing through the cracks*

While I was at CNS, we would have monthly conferences with my whole team on Zoom where my primary therapists take turns breaking down what's going on with my treatment. What's going well? What isn't working right? What should I incorporate into my home life?

During the November 2021 meeting, my case manager announced that I would be wrapping up my therapy time with CNS as the year ended. My goal for a long time had been to finish up therapy by the end of 2021. I didn't want to take it with me into 2022.

I thought it was a distant fantasy though; I never thought it would actually happen. In preparation, I started going to rehab four days a week instead of every weekday like I had been doing for almost two years. I was ready to move on.

I'm very grateful for CNS, and simultaneously, I think it is crazy that there's a demand for a place like it. It's shockingly sad how many people get serious brain injuries. I've met people as young as 19 with whole lives ahead to live. I've even seen little kids in the physical therapy gym.

I mean, I'm not this old lady; I was 22 when the accident happened and 26 when I finished writing this book—I also have a whole life to live ahead of me.

The people I met and saw younger than me at CNS made me sad. My injuries made me sad too, but it was a different feeling. Self-sympathy and empathy. They pull on different heartstrings.

It's been a long road. When I first started at CNS, they did a series of cognitive admission tests on me. They found my short-term memory to be in the second percentile. Meaning I only performed better than two percent of the population.

Six months later, I was in the 19th percentile for short-term memory, which was considered low-average in terms of immediately processing new information and retaining unfamiliar concepts. I was slowly improving in storing information in my brain.

My language was considered high average from very low six months before. My reasoning skills were considered average, up from very low, in the .3 percentile, on admission. However, I still needed to work on fluid reasoning, generalizing, and applying prior learning to new situations.

Before I was released from CNS, I retook a bunch of tests I did on my first day there, like looking at pictures identifying the hazards and pointing at specific parts of my body. One of the tests was drawing a picture of a person, not just a stick figure.

After I had drawn a person, my therapist gasped and asked if I wanted to see how I drew a person when I first got to CNS: It was a blob on top of more blobs with no hands. It was to tell how much body awareness I had. The one I had drawn now even had ears. It was much more identifiable as a human person.

My right hand can do the same work as my left when figuring out a cognitive task. Also, according to a six-minute walk around the clinic, I can cross a busy street and, ironically, not get hit by a car.

I made significant, fast gains, and I still have work to do. Might have to continue working for the rest of my life.

"I Can See," by Mac Miller sums it all up perfectly: "You got so far to go, but look at where you came from."[28]

Mac Miller has always been a favorite artist of mine. Newer Mac—*Circles* and *Swimming*, not *K.I.D.S.* or *Best Day Ever*.[29] He's been my favorite since high school, and in a morbidly ironic twist, he died on September 7th 2018, a year before I was injured.

Therapy at CNS is always working toward life after CNS. No one knows what a future life for me will look like. We are extremely hopeful that it'll keep getting better. I'm paradoxically lucky and unlucky.

Unlucky because I got hit by a car. Lucky because there was a nurse and a paramedic very close by when I was struck. Lucky because of the doctors and therapists I've been assigned to, and the opportunities I've been able to participate in because I live in Los Angeles. I mean, we live 15 to 20 minutes away from CNS. There are few places like it.

---

28   *Mac Miller – I can see*. (n.d.). Genius. https://genius.com/Mac-miller-i-can-see-lyrics
29   *Mac Miller - Discography*. (n.d.). Album of the Year. https://www.albumofthe-year.org/artist/2442-mac-miller/

During my recovery, therapists asked me cognitive questions while walking and doing the agility ladder to help prepare me for the real world. They asked me about the similarities between:

- Hospitals and pharmacies
- A grocery store and a restaurant.
- A clothing store and my closet.

My team knew I'd walk and talk to people simultaneously in the real world.

I used to play Jenga against other patients while balancing on some sort of balance board. There was a question on the back of every Jenga piece we pulled. It would ask us things like naming the capital of California, listing three activities at CNS, what you might buy at a grocery store.

All the therapists there trained in at least one other field. So, as a result, they had us doing or trying crazy things. Things that combined what I needed to work on. Or what everyone needed to work on. They did things that crossed disciplines for everyone.

CNS was my job. Except I didn't get paid. I went there every day for a few hours. I've made friends with some other patients there because I'm friendly, we're near each other, and I had to wake up early for it.

I feel like I went to grad school on how to be a "typical" person again. Except instead of a degree at the end of all this, I know how to walk and talk way better than I did before I went there.

In Spring 2021, I took over a mile walks alone around my neighborhood, sometimes with my doggy friend, Otis. At first, Diana was a little worried about me walking alone. I earnestly reassured her. I hadn't been alone for so long.

I wasn't going to allow Diana's fear to stop me from finally being alone. I've always been a big walker. Every day with Ted. For his good and my own.

Walking calms me down. It puts me into good head space. To be alone with my thoughts for about 20-plus minutes. I just walked around the neighborhood basically in circles; my neighborhood was a bunch of cul-de-sacs.

Sometimes, if I wasn't having the best day, I walked up to two and a half miles. That was my longest walk at the time. I have the best thoughts on my walks.

My brain works the best it can while I'm walking. It isn't to walk prettier or to hone down my gait, it's just solely for me. Probably one of the only things I have that doesn't benefit anyone else.

In May 2021, I started shopping again. Mostly grocery shopping because I am a foodie, and it excites me.

Diana would drop me off in front of a grocery store and I'd go in alone, armed with my reusable bags. I started with a small market that would be easier to navigate.

I shopped off the list I had created and just perused things around the store. I took in just a certain amount of money to help me learn to budget as I shopped so I had enough for when I checked out.

I can't drive right now or ever. So, Diana acts as my chauffeur and I'm great at Ubering. She drove me to and from CNS and to all my appointments.

I think it's morbidly funny that I was hit by a car, and now I can't drive a car. I know it's more complicated than that, but just thinking about how I am in this situation because of a driver and now I can't be a driver is infuriatingly ironic.

My recovery cost so much money.

The hospitals billed over $1.5 million to the insurance company in the first six months, which didn't even yet include the costs for CNS! It included ambulance rides, hospital stays, doctors, tests.

The insurance companies didn't pay that much, and of course, I haven't either. It illustrates that I'm expensive.

I was a preemie, born two months early, so I was in the NICU for three weeks. That alone resulted in a quarter of a million dollars being billed. In 1997.

It's 20-something years later. Unfortunately, things, especially medical services, just get more expensive as time goes on.

I'm not done recovering. My brain is still healing. My body is still healing. People tell me how amazing my recovery is and that the speed of it is surprising. It's still happening though. This is not how the rest of my life will be spent.

why did this happen?
why did who ever choose this?
I don't understand

chapter 21

reflections on a life turned upside down

one thing i could keep
is how much i love to write
especially now

September 7, 2019, changed my whole life. Flipped everything upside down for the rest of my life.

It does get easier in all ways: physically, I get stronger and more able-bodied.

It's crazy to reflect. I'm beyond grateful to everyone who has stood by me during this ordeal. Every therapist and doctor who has worked with me. I know it's their job, but it still means a lot to me.

Especially now, as my brain continues to heal, I'm becoming more aware. I am even more grateful to everyone who has helped me since I was hit by that car.

I technically graduated from college in May 2019. I had my graduation party and participated in a graduation ceremony at my school, with my friends and family attending.

I got a fake diploma because I still had two classes to finish, my capstone and a sustainable agriculture class for my environmental studies major. At the time of the accident, I was taking those two classes and a ceramics class for fun.

I started doing ceramics in college. I started throwing (that's the wheel) because my roommate at the time was super into it and one of my closest friends was trying to make a living out of it. So I was, by default, super into it.

I even worked on a volunteer basis at the kiln on campus. About four of us worked at it and slept overnight to fire the ceramics. I started doing that toward the beginning of my last year. I had done it a few times by the time I was hit by a car.

After our accident, my college advisor, who happened to be the head of the environmental studies department, worked with higher-ups at the university to substitute my last two classes with other things I had done so I wouldn't have to enroll back in school again.

Thank goodness they did that because I don't think I would have been able to go back to college and sit through two more classes. Learning about some people's theoretical pain would be next to impossible when I was going through so much of my real and traumatic pain.

I had a few goals, some that were short-term and some that were long-term. I tried to plan the next five years of my life. That is impossible, though.

So, I planned out what I could try for. I planned a little party with everyone on "Team Emily" to show my deep gratitude and love for them all.

For a while, I was planning on returning and being in Arcata for the second anniversary of my accident. But that would have been too much for me, and COVID had taken over the world.

I made a new plan to go back to Arcata in February 2022. To consciously say goodbye to that place and spread Ted's ashes among the redwoods, on the marsh in town, our favorite place to walk together, and on the beach up north because those were his favorite places.

Since numbers are so important to me, I decided to return to Arcata with Xenia, a former roommate and forever best friend, and to be there on 2/22/2022. She came for emotional support.

Speaking of emotional support, if Teddy had another favorite person, it was her. My love of synchronistic numbers flourished with her as my friend and housemate. Together, we planned the visit to serve as a beautiful ending to my sad story. A beautiful finale to my long, terrible story with that place.

I sat in the passenger seat of a car for 9+ hours to get to Northern California. We took our time traveling up the coast. We met up for breakfast with Jill, my therapist, on the way up. I hadn't seen her in person since before my accident.

We stayed in an Airbnb in Arcata, right in the middle of town, behind one of the grocery stores. We spread Teddy's ashes on the town's marsh. That was Teddy's favorite place to walk.

Saying goodbye to Teddy in Arcata brought me some closure I never got with him or with that place. It brought my healing about Teddy's death full circle. I can never change what happened.

I plan to fertilize a tree one day with the remainder of his ashes wherever I settle down. It'll be like a gift from him.

I don't know medically why I'm healing the way I am, instead of like the other people I saw at CNS who were healing much more slowly than me. I credit it all to him. He used the last little bit of his energy to see me through this thing.

My goal was to get a new dog on September 7, 2022. Instead, I brought Pepper home on April 4, 2022. About six weeks after we got back from Arcata. She shifted my emotional healing.

She is small enough to be picked up easily, which was a necessity. She has salt-and-pepper-speckled fur, not white. She is a girl, not a boy. She is far away from who Teddy was. I don't love her anymore or any less than Teddy; I have a completely different love for her.

I am hard on myself. Way harder than anyone else is. It's a big deal to everyone when I do anything successfully. I think I am hard on myself because I have really high expectations.

That was part of why I am not worse off than I was. But what scares me is that this injury won't go away even if I fully heal physically.

We will always be changed and marked by the things that happen in our lives. I can't heal 100% from getting hit by a car.

This isn't something I'll eventually get over. It's going to be a lifelong struggle. I heard stories of people suffering from traumatic brain injuries, losing their ability to walk and talk, and then a few years later, you'd never guess they had a brain injury.

Part of me likes hearing stories like that. Part of me hates it. I never knew what the extent of their injuries were, or what their rehab program was like.

I don't think that there are many places in the world as comprehensive in terms of a rehab program as CNS. So as far as I know, which is not very far at all, none of these people who recovered were getting the same level of care as I did.

I hope so hard that one day people will say, "I'd have never known just looking at you and talking to you that you've had a traumatic brain injury." That's all it is now, a hope for the future. That it will look a whole lot different than the present moment.

Yes, I know I will have this for the rest of my life. Hopefully, it gets to the point that people can't tell anymore.

I know every injury and people's bodies are different, and I am very grateful because I see firsthand how much worse this thing could have been.

I also know how hard it was for so long. Not to be able to walk on my own. Or to type. Or to have my cognitive level be where it is. Or even to go to the restroom on my own.

They were all my reality at some point. It was very hard to be faced with that every day. It makes me feel weird, but very grateful.

My speech therapist urgently called me into her office one day. She said she had something important for me. She played a recording on her phone of me describing a picture when I first started at CNS.

The recording she played was of someone talking quietly and mumbling every word they said. Unrecognizable as me. It was like I was listening to a completely different person talking.

I was feeling down on myself before she played that recording for me, like this whole process was taking forever.

Hearing that impressed me and made me proud of how far I'd come.

I've talked a lot about my physical and cognitive healing processes, but a huge part of my recovery that I've only touched on is emotional healing. Some days, I get really sad. As I get cognitively better, all I've lost since even before 2019 really hits me.

Writing this chapter of the book was even pretty emotional for me. When I consider everything I've lost, I just get overwhelmed. My rehab, losing Teddy, the insurance company denying me, or having to re-organize everything in my life.

I cry easily. I always have.

Sometimes, I get stuck on a horrible thought and can't get rid of it. The horrible what-ifs of life, like, what if I can never walk "normally" again? Or what if my right arm can never straighten out fully? What if I can never dream again?

It's a vicious circle. One day, I was thinking, for the first time ever, and I don't know why it came into my head, about Teddy being cremated, being burned. I know he couldn't feel it, but I kept thinking about his little body burning. Until there was nothing left. Just ashes. My therapist thinks that it was a sign of me healing emotionally.

Occasionally, I get super sad and angry. When this happens, my voice gets progressively louder to the point that I almost shout. I have been told that my moods are natural, especially when I'm hormonal.

Angry, I blurt out hurtful things and lash out at family and friends. I had days when I just wanted to die and would say it would have been better if I had died the day of the accident.

I am suffering from depression and anxiety since being hit. I still talk to my therapist once a week on Tuesdays, and during difficult periods we talk twice a week.

At first, my neurologist prescribed Lexapro to help level out my moods. I took it at dinner then switched to the morning because I don't need to be in a stable mood while sleeping.

I later started working with a psychiatrist who added Wellbutrin to my daily pills. That helped with the depression. He keeps tweaking the dosage, upping one and reducing the other.

Hopefully, we will find the right combination. The antidepressant and anxiety medication combo became honestly a lifesaver for me. It can change how I'm feeling chemically.

All my therapists at CNS told me that brain healing ebbs and flows, especially when you've already re-learned how to walk and talk. After that, the healing is happening at a much more complex level. You can't see it as easily.

So, sometimes I feel like I'm not getting better, although my voice is normalizing in cadence and people have commented on my gait improving. When you do the healing, it is hard to see the changes. It seemed infinitesimal when we were doing tele-rehab.

I know it was for everyone's health, and the pandemic was so hard on everyone, but I got so frustrated doing rehab through the computer. It made everything seem so slow.

That being said, not all changes are bad; but I have trouble looking at my life from that perspective. So I went to Diana to ask how it had changed me.

She said that before the accident, I was stubborn to a fault, and sometimes I was hardheaded. But now, I have turned that stubbornness into a good thing. I never give up, and I always keep working.

I used to close myself off out of stubbornness and pride. Diana says now I'm open with my feelings, I ask for help when I need it, I'm able to apologize and understand when I've done something wrong, and I'm more ready to express gratitude when someone helps me.

My recovery also highlighted my ability to figure out how to get things done. Even though some things are a little bit harder for me now, or I do them a little bit slower, I still find a way to complete whatever I'm trying to do, whether it is cooking, showering, or walking around. My aunt stressed that it has highlighted my resilience and perseverance.

Diana said I have been beaten down by life and thrown more than my fair share of challenges, but I don't allow anything to win over me. I was tough before and have dealt with tragedy already, but I'm even tougher now.

I won't let this defeat me. I have chosen to fight back.

I don't want my TBI to always be at the forefront of everything I talk about. It has started to happen. I'll be the first to admit, I bring up the accident a lot. To try to make it light-hearted and funny.

It was this extremely heavy thing that happened to me. So, I attempt to talk about it casually. I realize I'm trying to make it more of a commonplace thing. I know my family and friends don't need a reminder that I was hit by a freaking car. You don't forget that.

Recently, in the dentist's waiting room, with the pale blue walls, I listened to the receptionist ask Diana if there had been any changes to my medical history in the last two years since I'd been there.

She replied almost too casually that I had suffered from a traumatic brain injury since I'd last been there. It's still impossibly hard and awkward to hear my neurological status being discussed offhandedly. Then again, it's a result of things getting better, and not having my TBI always be the first thing to discuss, so I guess that's progress.

At the end of 2020, I wrote holiday cards to Barlow Hospital, Texhoma, and Northridge rehab staff. I couldn't write more than one in a sitting because my hand would get tired, so my writing would get messy. I wrote the same thing to all three places. I wrote, "Happy holidays!!! Thank you so much for caring for me when I most needed it. I'll never forget y'all (even if I don't remember being there). Thanks to you, I'm showering alone, walking, cooking, and writing this letter, and I'm like 80% better. I owe my recovery to you all. I'll forever be indebted to you."

On June 8, 2022, it was a Wednesday, I visited Barlow Hospital again, but consciously this time. The head of their PR department had emailed my aunt, explaining how every time they see the Christmas card I wrote to their staff, they think about me and wanted to know if I was up for an interview for a small promotional video.

On camera, it was Dr. Kashani (the wonderful doctor who was in charge of my care during my stay there), Diana, and me. The filming crew also took the B-roll of us talking and hugging the nurses. In the rough final cut the PR department sent Diana, my doctor said that my return served as a reminder of why he had become a doctor.

Here's what they asked:

- What was I doing? I told them I was discharged from rehab but still working on physical therapy and taking classes online through UCLA;

- What was the darkest part of my recovery? I said I wished I had died alongside Teddy that fateful Sunday; and

- What had been the brightest moment in my recovery? I said I was very grateful that Teddy took the brunt of the car's impact and that I lived to see September 8, 2019.

The editors of the interview took out my answer to the question about my darkest times. My answer had been too real and dark for their video. The focus was on healing.

They inserted pictures we provided, and it ends with Pepper and me in my life post-Barlow. You can see it on You-Tube if you search for Barlow Hospital Emily Owen.[30]

I lived at Barlow Hospital for six weeks, and more than two years later, I met a handful of nurses who had worked with me and were still there.

I met my former team of physical therapists and some of the doctors who had made sure I made it through. It was unbelievably intense, and tears were shed.

To see this team of people who had tirelessly worked to keep me safe when they didn't even know me was extremely powerful. I told them about my book and Pepper while promising a future return to do a book signing for them.

---

30   *Emily Owen | Barlow Respiratory Hospital.* (n.d.). Barlow Respiratory Hospital. https://barlowhospital.org/patient-stories/emily/

Seeing these people made me speechless. I didn't know what to say. "Thank you," just didn't seem to cover it. I gave countless hugs. I told them all if they ever needed anything in the future, even a ride to the airport, I would make it work to show my gratitude.

I left after a few hours of chatting and hugging. I was feeling so loved and taken care of. I knew that seeing me walking and talking after I could barely open my eyes while I was a patient there made their day, too. Maybe their week, month, and maybe even their year.

Patients don't often return to acknowledge the ones who are there early on in their recoveries. I left there feeling so good that I got to show them how I was doing.

every day is
a gift. i am so grateful for
everything i see

chapter 22

reclaiming my life

my piercings are back
i'm feeling more like myself
slowly coming back

This has been a long journey. Hopefully just a speed bump in my life. Except instead of a regular speed bump, it's one of those long, gently sloping ones.

I'm editing this chapter in September 2023. The four-year anniversary of our accident just passed, with little to no fanfare. Four years of desperately trying to hold onto some sense of selfhood.

My best friend, Xenia, came to spend the day with me so I wouldn't be alone. We walked Pepper almost six miles, went to a vegetarian taco place to have lunch, and spent the day focusing on love and delicious tacos.

I began writing this book in March 2020. I was alert enough to want to write a book but couldn't even walk alone or write my name. I dictated the first few chapters to my aunt.

I thought of writing a book to tell my story, but I couldn't type it for a while. I could only speak in a whisper at the time. A few months in, once I'd tackled typing, I would write every day when I got home from rehab and on some weekends. At first, I only wrote for maybe an hour at the most. I would need cues to write more and longer.

"How did that make you feel?"

"What were you thinking at that point?"

"What do you remember from that time?"

My original intention when it was clear I was writing a book, this book, was for it to be 22 chapters. I was 22 when the accident happened. It made sense. As I wrote more and more, I realized there needed to be another chapter and then another chapter. Originally, this chapter was called 'The Process of Writing this Book."

I realized it was more than just an account of the process. It became the story of me getting my life back. The updated title of this chapter comes from when Diana had just be-grudgingly driven me to the dispensary.

She wondered what my mom would say if she could see us. I responded with "She'd be happy, like, 'Go, baby, reclaim your life!'" Also, my story didn't end at 22.

This book was finally finished when I was 26, and I hope I have many years ahead. I ended up with 26 chapters.

Parts of the last chapters of this book, unlike the others, were written in real time. As things happened to me, I added them to the book. So, I sometimes move back and forth be-tween the past and present tense.

Throughout the process of writing this book, some days I would write several whole pages, and others I would only be able to write one, two, or three paragraphs, tops.

Some days, I could type for hours until my aunt came and asked when I would be done. Others, I would only write for a matter of minutes. It depended on the day and how much had happened.

meeting the real world, virtually

IN JANUARY 2021, I STARTED TO VENTURE INTO THE REAL world, trying to normalize my life beyond just going to rehab. It was online, but it was my first non-clinical experience outside of a hospital or rehab since the accident.

My cognitive rehab therapist, Victoria, suggested that I take some writing classes. We found a writing workshop online hosted by LA Writers Group.

There was a maximum of eight people allowed in the class per session. I was feeling trepidation the first few weeks about sharing that I was hit by a car. The group of eight people was the largest with whom I had shared my story.

They handled it very kindly. I mean, you can't really handle someone sharing with you that they were hit by a car in any way but with compassion, concern, and empathy.

Unless you're a sociopath.

Before I started the class, we didn't know if I had the attention skills to be in a class for almost three hours, but I did.

In the class, the facilitator would give us prompts, and then we would write for ten or fifteen minutes. We could choose to share if we felt called to. Most of the time, I got a few paragraphs that I added into this book after the class. That class helped me add details and descriptions beyond just recounting facts, to put everything in my own words.

It was nice to get feedback from people who weren't living my story. It was also cool to share my story with new people. To tell them exactly what had happened to me. You can't necessarily tell just by looking at me.

Throughout the first almost-two years after my accident, I didn't feel like I looked like myself without my piercings. All my piercings were taken out to get me into the MRI machine. My dad had to look on the internet for how to remove a nose piercing because no one there at the time could do it.

I finally got my ears re-pierced on May 29, 2021. It hurt, but I've discovered that my pain tolerance is much higher now. Also, the piercer only had to reopen three of the holes. Four of them were stubborn and stayed open.

My nose piercings had completely closed almost immediately, and I couldn't get them pierced again yet because of the pandemic; I had to keep my mask on. A piercing shop I found online offered to pierce my nose after hours and under the table, but I waited until I could go there openly to get them pierced.

meeting the real world again ... for real

VICTORIA, MY FORMER COGNITIVE REHAB THERAPIST, TOLD ME to start thinking about my future, what I want to do, and where I want to be. She said that therapy could and should just fit into my life.

We talked about doing things I enjoyed, volunteering, and forging a life outside my little therapy world. We also talked about the timing of the pandemic.

I expressed that I was happy the pandemic didn't hit while I was in the hospital. I already hated my time in hospitals, even with someone there 75% of the time, 90% of the time when I was awake. At least I wasn't alone and lonely on top of everything else.

So, I started venturing out into the world, this time in person instead of online. I had taken ceramics classes in college. I loved it and the whole firing process; it was like cooking in a weird way.

It was cathartic, so I researched pottery classes near my house and found an option. It was only a ten-minute drive from where I lived and could easily fit into my therapy schedule especially now that they were slowly starting to lessen my hours there.

The ceramic class was from 3 to 5 p.m. every Monday in July. Before my first class, I had my occupational therapist email the instructor.

She compared it to if you had an ear infection and decided to take a swim class, you would tell the instructor. More of a heads-up than an appeal for modifications. For my first experience in person, out of a clinical setting, I wanted a professional detailing my deficits.

My hands don't work as well together *yet* as they used to. Hopefully, it's just *not yet*. It was very disheartening. I still gave it a good try but quickly realized my hands weren't doing what I wanted them to, although they were slowly reaching into the muscle memory they once knew.

I went outside the class hours to give it a go without my teacher closely observing me. Going alone, and flying solo, it went okay. I switched the wheel from the traditional right-hand dominant spinning to left-hand dominant. So it spun to the left instead of to the right.

I figured that regardless of which hand I write with, my left hand is the more dominant. I mostly ate with my left hand, wiped after I went to the restroom with my left hand, and I buttoned buttons with my left hand.

the world of work

At Victoria's request, and with Diana's help, I prepared an updated resume in the summer of 2021. To sort of have a leg-up for when I'm prepared to reenter the real world.

Since then, it's become clear that **this** is my calling. Writing books, sharing my stories. Not everyone can write a whole book. The dedication and commitment. Writing a book is working on the same project for YEARS.

Sam called it my elevator pitch. My way of describing what happened to me in a way that is easily understood and easy for me to explain. I think forever it'll be hard for me to explain my accident. To explain my brain injury as a result of being hit by a car when I was 22. When this book finally becomes available to the public, not just the people I send this google doc to.

Forever. Never. In my whole life. I think in absolute terms. I shouldn't, though. Everything is temporary, and I know that, but I can't help it. I struggle to live in the moment these days. I'm always stuck at least a year in the future. Sometimes a theoretical five years into the future.

Living in the now or in the moment anymore is a struggle. My present moment could be a lot worse, but it isn't great. I can't just accept that this is it. I won't accept it.

I think that is one of the main reasons my recovery is going how it has. I refuse to accept anything less than how I want to live the rest of my life.

I got a job toward the end of 2021. My first post-college and post-injury job. My first real-world, official job. As the communications director—really more of a glorified social media specialist—for a renewable energy company.

My dad worked for them, so that's how I heard about it; but I still had to send them a resume and interview. Although I did get inside information, there was barely any nepotism involved.

I only worked ten hours a week. It was a huge accomplishment. It was time to see if I could apply everything I've learned in therapy. They talked a lot about turning the real world into my therapy because research and reading at a job can take over for cognitive rehab.

It was a good work experience in a safe and cushioned environment, but it only lasted a few months because I wasn't ready. But you don't know until you try.

discharge

FROM THE END OF JUNE THROUGH MID-JULY 2021, WE WORKED on my discharge testing for educational therapy and cognitive rehab. I'm assuming a team of professionals created this set of tests. I guess I took them once for my intake. I have no memory of this, but all my rehab programs aim to show improvement. There is no pass or fail in rehab.

Educational testing had multiple parts. Math, which is broken up into a few sections such as multiplication, square roots, and geometry. There's also addition and subtraction, and then it becomes impossible with trigonometry and calculus, things I don't even remember learning in school.

Vocabulary and reading comprehension was basically just filling in the blank. Other tests measured my written language skills. The tests are designed for a wide range of people to complete them. That's why there were some annoyingly easy questions and some annoyingly hard questions.

Other testing measured my cognitive abilities in six areas: working memory, long-term retrieval, fluid reasoning, comprehension-knowledge processing speed, and cognitive efficiency. In the first four areas I showed marked improvement but in the last two I remained low.

In cognitive rehab (CR), I had to be given the discharge testing with the same person who gave it to me initially. So, I was assigned to Victoria for a couple of days of testing. She hadn't usually seen patients since becoming the director of rehab. I was a little surprised to see her initials on my schedule.

The testing was all over the place; some timed math and general knowledge information. Some crossing words out, naming certain things, and being able to think of the correct term for a certain image.

She also gave me an assessment where I had to tell her the opposite of certain words. Regardless of brain injury, I'm a fairly intelligent person, but I'd never even heard half of the words I was presented with!

The tests aren't designed for someone with a brain injury. Or even any injury at all. They are a set of standardized tests given to everyone from toddlers to Ph.D. candidates.

When Victoria delivered my results, they showed I was now in the average range! Low average for numerical processing, high average for deductive reasoning, and superior in my ability to regurgitate information I was told.

We compared my scores on these cognitive tests to my scores the other two times I had completed this testing — when I first started with CNS almost two years earlier, in March 2020, and after I had done the TMS tapping (transcranial magnetic stimulation) at UCLA in November 2020.

Most of my initial scores were very low, with some below the first percentile. Leaving, I even had some scores in the superior range. I continued to have low scores in all math areas, but I was never very good in math so that didn't bother me much. My highest score was in written language and represented my biggest strength, all in line with my skills before the accident.

I was supposed to be discharged from cognitive rehab at the end of August 2021. Every time discharge was brought up, I would either tear up or full-on cry.

The thought of leaving CR and not making any improvement on my own scared me, but they wouldn't suggest it without confidence in my cognitive abilities. I'm pretty confident in my cognitive abilities, and I think I am close to where I was in my way of thinking pre-accident. I am just a very rigid thinker. Not flexible at all. I process and respond slower than before, but my underlying skills remain.

I was so anxious about leaving CR. It turned into a very slow goodbye which helped lessen my anxiety. My daily sessions went down to every other day, then twice a week. Finally, I was down to just one day a week of cognitive therapy.

I'd basically completed all of the cognitive tasks, for example, rearranging sentences in alphabetical order, reverse alphabetical order, and shortest to longest word. Which is actually really hard. Especially doing it all in my head. If they were the same length of letters, I would have to alphabetize them.

Since I had leveled out of almost everything, cognitive therapy became the more traditional form of speech therapy. My weekly sessions worked on my vocalization. They became essentially about doing my AAHHH's for longer and louder.

Visually, you can't easily tell that something traumatic happened to me. My deficits show only when you zoom into my walking patterns and bilateral coordination (my ability to use both hands symmetrically). It's really my speech patterns and voice that clued people in. I talked slowly and in a low voice. It was often somewhat robotic.

Talking more often is the best therapy for that. It's a good thing that I can't shut up. However, it's still the thing that will key people in that something terrible happened to me. My voice has a lower tone than it did. I didn't know if it was from the intubation messing up my vocal cords or maybe the trach affected my vocal folds.

My speech therapists had recommended that I see an ear, nose, and throat doctor (an ENT) just to be sure there was nothing physically wrong with me. We found one at UCLA, and they saw no damage, just slight calluses on my vocal cords.

In preparation for my discharge, I started to give away the splints and other tools like the adaptive kitchen utensils that helped me in my recovery. Since insurance will some-times refuse to pay for equipment and even therapy, I wanted to be sure others had the same opportunities for recovery I did. Most of what I used stayed in the hospital where I used it, and Hearts in Motion received my wrist and leg splints.

Victoria got my "yes" and "no" buttons, to pass along to another new patient. They can be, and have been, helpful in communicating to others how you're feeling when you oth-erwise can't tell them.

She also got these old emoji balls, one with a huge smile and another crying. I never used them. I much preferred the thumbs up, thumbs down method of communicating. She also now has laminated paper sheets with doodles of a toilet, a bed, and a cup of water because keeping them made me sad by reminding me of a time when I needed help to communicate.

this is my life now,
hurt for a little while more
but not forever

chapter 23

life after discharge

i like the patterns
makes things more interesting
synchronicity

As we prepared for my life after my discharge, my occupational therapist asked me what prevented me from living a fulfilling life. I told her my lack of driving ability was a huge thing. I also mentioned camping.

She asked me why I couldn't camp. I didn't have a reason besides there wasn't anyone other than my dad to camp with, and camping with my dad is a whole different story.

One of my closest friends, Shanti, would be coming into town for my September 7, 2021, celebration to celebrate my life, so I planned to camp then. I figured that was the perfect time to sleep outside.

My dad bought me the easiest pop-up tent from Amazon, and I already had a sleeping bag that would keep me warm enough. We had a great time. We weren't allowed to make a fire because we were in the middle of fire season, but we had a blast fire-free.

It was fantastic to know that I am still capable of going camping. I now know that I should, and will in the future, ask to be closer to a bathroom; we were far from it, and every time I had to pee it was a trek, and at that time I really shouldn't have been wandering out alone.

While sleeping outside, I felt more like myself than I had in two years. Camping was a huge thing for me because I loved sleeping on the ground. I do like a bed. It's way more comfortable, and sleeping in a sleeping bag makes you appreciate the bed.

I got tipsy to the point of drunkenness while playing Scrabble. My favorite things were coming together: the outdoors, Scrabble, and sharing a bottle of wine with a very close friend.

I went to a wedding for a family friend. I was determined to make it as "normal" as possible. I wore black wedges because wedges are a lot sturdier than heels. Way easier than heels. I had also broken my foot during my recovery. I took my wedges into physical therapy to practice in them before I had to wear them.

Since I knew the wedding was outside, Janki had me practice wearing the wedges over unsteady ground to prepare for walking over grass. She laid out a ton of the weights you strap to your ankles, then covered them with yoga mats, and told me to walk over them.

I couldn't see where they were, and it forced me to walk slowly and cautiously so I wouldn't trip on them. They told me I couldn't wear heels because of my balance issues. So, I wore wedges, trying to gain some more normalcy, like I was conquering every mountain.

In another attempt to grasp normalcy and return it to my life, I went to San Diego to visit Xenia, another one of my best friends. I took the Amtrak train by myself. It was a huge step towards independence. Due to the pandemic and my deficits, I hadn't been there by myself yet.

I learned my new limits on that trip. Xenia and I went to the beach and traversed the rocky slopes that were like a balance beam in real life. I could do it successfully, but it wasn't the easiest for me and I made my way through very slowly.

Climbing is not the easiest. Other people were jogging up and lapping me. It was treacherous but doable. My balance is getting better, but it was still tough for me. I think having to stand on just one leg and hopping from rock to rock is hard for anybody.

Before I left, Diana and I went to a huge but familiar mall to prepare for my trip. I navigated through the mall by myself, going to certain stores, and buying a few things, while keeping in mind what time I was supposed to meet up with my aunt so we could go home together.

I got carried away and met up with her later than I was supposed to because I struggled with time management. But I did it without getting lost!

The train ride itself had gone very well. I sat on the lower level so I wouldn't have to navigate the stairs. The porter helped me on and off the train. I made friends with the older woman sitting next to me on the way there.

The only hiccup was when we got to San Diego, I bent down to pick up my book that I had dropped. I didn't put enough weight on my right foot and fell. Not very far, but still. My whole side of the train crowded around me to ask if I was okay. I was fine, but my pride was bruised.

On the way home, the train back was postponed for a few hours because the train had hit a pedestrian at the stop before mine. This news really shook me up. Getting hit by a car sucks, and I wouldn't recommend it to anyone, but it's better than getting hit by a train.

The train workers said we were postponed because they had to clean up the "human remains." So, my friend had to drive me from Northern San Diego to Los Angeles. We ended up having a good time as travel buddies, and we had a moment for the human who had lost their life to the train just miles away from where we were.

driving was my final frontier

I STRUGGLE WITH ATTENTION, AND MY VISION IS NOW SIGNIFI-cantly poorer than before the accident. Also, my reflexes aren't as fast as they should be to be able to safely get behind the wheel of a car. I hoped that by the end of 2021, I would be able to drive once again.

I read some very scary statistics regarding elevated risks for crashes after a TBI. However, the results of studies are mixed, without uniform criteria.

Between 50-70% of people who have suffered from a TBI, return to driving and in one study done in Italy, 63% of those with severe traumatic brain injury who then started driving again were then involved in car accidents.[31]

I also know from my therapists at CNS who warned me that people who have suffered from one traumatic brain in-

---

31   Schultheis, M. T., & Whipple, E. K. (2014). Driving after Traumatic Brain Injury: evaluation and rehabilitation interventions. *Current Physical Medicine and Rehabilitation Reports*, 2(3), 176–183. https://doi.org/10.1007/s40141-014-0055-0

jury are 40% more likely to suffer from a second one. Those unlucky enough to get two TBIs are 80% more likely to get a third!

That being acknowledged, my neuro-optometrist told me we could look at driving at the end of 2021. I talked to him and my occupational therapist about being prepared to not drive at night and only travel on comfortable, close roads.

My night vision is seriously impaired, and it feels better on roads I know well. Especially when I first got behind the wheel again.

I was enrolled in Drive Focus, an online driving program to try to reach my driving goal in occupational therapy and at home. It takes you through a first-person driving simulation where you identify all the potential hazards and traffic signs. I had to click on the stop signs, traffic lights, and pedestrians.

When you're done with a drive, the program rates you and tells you what you should have done differently. It also gives you your general reaction time, how long it takes you to react to a hazard.

My OT also gave me exercises to do while in the car with someone. It was called lighthouse scanning, where she wanted me to turn my head all the way to each side to fully see my surroundings.

At the same time, I had to perform various tasks like counting the number of lights, the number of pedestrians, the number of cars changing lanes, items starting with different letters of the alphabet. This was fun at first but soon felt like too much of a chore.

My OT and neuro-optometrist were working with me to reach my goal of driving again. We all decided I could sign up for driving rehab and start considering getting behind the wheel of a car by November 2021.

Around New Year's Eve 2020, I started visualizing driving to the beach in the coming years, potentially with my future little dog riding shotgun. But that hope turned out to be too optimistic.

I participated in about eight hours of behind-the-wheel training, and in mid-February 2022, the head of the driving rehab wanted to ride along during one of my lessons. To see how I was handling driving again.

We drove together for just fifteen minutes. She'd seen enough apparently. I couldn't pay enough attention and there were many safety barriers that would keep me from driving once again.

She recommended waiting, and letting my brain heal more. Allowing my eyes to adjust more to my glasses, and having my memory, attention, and reaction times improve. At that point, I accepted that driving was something much further in my future, if at all, and did not return for more rehab lessons.

saying good-bye to CNS was bittersweet

My last week at CNS was full of emotion. Full of hugs, discharge testing, and love. Sam got me a planner for the new year as my goodbye gift. To keep me on track. She said her parting message was, "Take it one day at a time," and to just have trust in the process.

There have been many days when I've panicked. *Would I ever get married? Would we have kids? Would I be able to drive those theoretical kids to school?*

It was time for my last PT sessions. In addition to a bunch of motor skill tests, I had to prove my ability to safely conduct myself in the community. I showed that I looked to both sides of me before crossing a street.

As I was walking out of the PT gym for my last time, Janki followed me out and said she wanted to stay in my story. She gave me her number and told me to wait a few weeks before I called.

For my last session of cognitive rehab, Victoria let me pick what we worked on. We redid a lot of my intake assessments to prove my growth, and I scored high on every one of them; sustained phonation (22 seconds, up from my previous high of 20), word fluency (24 words in 60 seconds, up from 20), and auditory memory (delayed recall at almost 100%).

I was excited and scared to tackle life (mostly) on my own. Thinking back, it was kind of insane to consider because I hadn't been solo for so long.

By the time I left, Hena had been discharged, and Derek wasn't there because they were weaning him off CNS. On my last day with Derek, he brought me a beautiful bouquet of flowers. To congratulate me. It was a bummer that my main rehabbing friends were not able to be at CNS for my last day, but it still felt like it was a huge day.

I got a certificate of completion from CNS signed by all the staff there. Even a few names of people I'd never met. All wishing me luck on this next chapter of my life.

My therapists gave me a t-shirt, a reusable water bottle, and some handwritten cards. Just from the ones I really had developed a relationship with. I passed all the discharge testing goals and surpassed most of the numbers they'd expected me to reach.

It rained during my first week at CNS and it rained most of my last week there, too. It doesn't rain often in Los Angeles. So it was a weird coincidence.

I'm a very spiritual person. I'm just not faithful in a g-d or a religion, organized way. It's more of a numbers, coincidences, and reoccurrences. I try to go to sleep at 11:11 and I love whenever I see a 333 or 555 or 777, any set of repeating numbers. I know so many people, literally not figuratively, all over the world were praying for me.

> the future scares me
> it exists in a timeline
> we're just not there yet

chapter 24

lost salt, found pepper

my dog will know ted
they'll be different to me,
never replace him

I was discharged! Real life was finally starting again.

To get back in the swing of things, I enrolled in two UCLA online extension classes. Since I was finishing up college at the time of my accident, it seemed like a good way to reenter the real world as a student. I signed up for two classes; one I dropped, and one I finished.

My life was on hold for a little while after leaving CNS. I felt as if I was on vacation. I got three weeks of just pure relaxation before starting the UCLA classes.

I was sleeping late most days, eating brunch (because I wasn't waking up early enough for both breakfast and lunch), and I was taking at least a mile-and-a-half walk around my neighborhood. Once a week, Otis would join me, but I would walk alone when he wasn't there.

Around the same time as I completed CNS, I started searching for a new furbaby. I would look on Petfinder almost daily. The idea of loving another dog was scary. Would they always live in Teddy's shadow?

It's remarkable how you feel when you lose one companion dog, to live and learn, realizing you can love another dog. Maybe not as much, and definitely not in the same way, but in a *different* way. In a way that just reminds you how big our hearts are and how infinite our capacity for love is.

It felt weird to think of getting a dog. Would I call them my second dog? My new dog? Another dog? Whoever that dog ended up being in my life, they'd never be Ted. I was scared that Teddy's ghost would think I was cheating on him.

He wasn't the friendliest to other dogs he met. Reflecting though, I think Teddy knew on some level that it was me or him. One of us had to go.

My active search for a little buddy started when I came home from spreading Teddy's ashes. I was looking at Petfinder's app almost every day. There is a shelter about a ten-minute drive from my house. The Los Angeles City East Valley Animal Shelter.

I went there twice and didn't find the right dog for me. I don't know what I expected. The perfect dog to just appear at the exact time I was looking?

I had gotten maybe three rejections from a few dogs I'd found through Petfinder. *"It isn't the right fit."* Or the dog had high energy, so they wanted the dog to be placed in a home with another dog. I was downhearted, so sad that I thought I was never going to find the right dog.

Was this Teddy telling me it was too soon? I didn't know, but I have always been an impatient person and I felt like

I was emotionally ready for a dog. Why wasn't one coming to me?

After many failed attempts on Petfinder, I saw that they offered another service through their sister website. Get Your Pet worked on rehoming pets whose parents couldn't take care of them anymore for some reason. I decided to browse their website and look at dogs near me that needed a new home.

Staring back at me through their website were these two beautiful, soulful brown eyes. They belonged to a small-enough-looking black-and-white dog named Pepper. I messaged her soon-to-be former owner and asked if I could meet up with her the following day to see how we got along.

She accepted my request, and we made a plan to meet up for the introduction in a local golf course's parking lot. She had recently relocated to Los Angeles from Pittsburgh for a job and told me that Pepper was a pandemic pup, which was great while she worked from home.

Now she was back at work, she didn't have the time or energy to give Pepper the life she deserved. The parking lot I chose was close to me, and apparently also to them.

My dad drove me since my aunt couldn't because of her mom's schedule. So much worked out the way it was supposed to. I was weirdly nervous on the way there. It felt a little like a blind date. My dad pulled up his car next to hers and we all got out.

Pepper was being carried and seemed terrified when she was put on the ground. Her owner at the time said Pepper was shy and would be timid at first.

I leaned down and knelt so we could make eye contact. I asked Pepper if she wanted to live with me. She didn't answer, but she let me hold her and leaned her head onto my shoulder, so I took that as a yes.

I showed her the tattoo of Teddy on my leg and said something along the lines of, "This is Teddy, your brother. You'll never be able to meet him, unfortunately, but I think you guys might have liked each other."

Pepper licked the tattoo, and I asked her former mom whether I could take her on a little walk first. We walked just to the other side of the parking lot and back. I was sold.

She was so flipping cute, apparently never barked, would never bite anyone, and slept through the night. She was the perfect next dog for me. The perfect size, quiet, cuddly, and more afraid of Diana than Diana would be of her.

We met up on a Saturday and we decided to wait until Monday to transfer ownership of Pepper so Pepper could say goodbye to her friends and family. Her owner also hadn't brought any of Pepper's things with her. She had a bed, some clothes, food, and bowls to pack up.

Those last two nights sleeping alone felt lonelier than ever. It gave me time to see Otis one more time without someone else stealing my attention. I was so ready to be a dog mom again. Pepper was the first dog I'd met and hopefully will be the dog for me for the next ten years or so.

I took Pepper home on April 4, 2022, two days after meeting her and a week before my birthday. She's the best birthday gift I've ever, and probably will ever, give to myself. I'm so beyond happy I did because she is perfect. She's only sixteen pounds so I can easily pick her up and carry her.

Diana has been afraid of dogs her whole life, but really took to Pepper. My whole life, we had to lock away the dogs if Diana was coming by the house.

When we decided that I would live at her house once we lost my mom, there was never a question whether Teddy would come with me. Then, when I broke my ankle in 2016, she would take Teddy on his twice daily walks.

Pepper's favorite spot to chill became under Diana's bed. Almost every time Pepper sees Diana, she lies down on her back, exposing her belly, waiting for tummy scratches.

Diana even helped me give Pepper a shower when she would get smelly—Pepper, not Diana. I soon decided that giving Pepper baths wasn't good for our relationship because she's so afraid of water; I didn't want to be associated with the dreaded shower or bath.

Pepper is the most perfect dog for me right now. The months before I adopted her, I wasn't sure what having a different dog would be like. She sleeps in my bed and snuggles up next to me all night long.

Then, she wakes up the second I open my eyes. Already excited for our morning walk, and her morning breakfast.

I wasn't sure I could love another dog again. I felt like a widow; finding another life partner was a scary thought. I spent many nights worried about my future dog.

What they would be like and how I would feel settling into an old routine of walking two or three times a day and remembering to feed another life form, to be totally responsible for another life. I quickly and comfortably fell back into the old habits.

When Pepper pees, she lifts a leg like a boy dog and when Teddy peed, he would squat like a girl. She actually does this weird combination of a squat while she is lifting a leg. Doesn't look easy and I don't know where she picked it up.

I am weirdly touched by the idea that they both pee like the opposite gender. He would squat and she lifts a leg.

Pepper keeps me grounded in this time and place. This moment. I know that I never would have met her had Teddy continued living. I don't think I would've had two small dogs at one time. I never would have sought her out.

She might've gone into the shelter system or ended up with a less fitting or deserving owner. She reminds me to stay present and grateful for this life I am living. Despite the traumas I've experienced and had to work through. Regardless of those traumas. In spite of those traumas.

At the end of May 2022, almost six months after I'd been discharged from CNS, I returned as an alumnus with my friend, Leili. I took Pepper so everyone could meet her.

I'm not sure who had the idea first, but we decided that we wanted to go back to CNS.

The rest of our little group that we meet up with from time to time, didn't want to visit or were still there as patients. We figured Leili's mom would drive us, so they picked us up on the way to the clinic.

We felt like celebrities as everyone said hello to us back in the clinic (and gave Pepper scratches). Victoria, Jellisa, Sam, and Janki were all excited to see us.

They were the only staff around whom we had worked with because there had been so many new hires since the end of 2021. Pepper got more love and scratches in the hour and a half we were there than she's gotten in her whole, short life so far.

I wasn't as motivated as I should have been after "graduating" out of CNS. I continued to work with Janki on Wednesdays until she switched jobs to another rehab clinic out of easy driving range. I then had a few months of chilling.

During this waiting limbo, a typical Friday for me was waking up after 9 and drinking my iced coffee with oat milk outside, soaking up the sun while watching Pepper explore our backyard, or sitting at our kitchen counter sipping my coffee and eating breakfast. I deserved the break-ish time while it lasted.

I was taking the occasional UCLA extension writing class online. I had shifted back to basically showering every day, doing my own laundry, and cooking dinner for our little four-person house on my self-proclaimed meatless Mondays.

I was walking Pepper mostly in circles around our neighborhood loop of two maybe three cul de sacs smushed together in the middle of Los Angeles. Pepper and I would also have the occasional walk to a nearby coffee shop. Sometimes we'd go on a walk with my dad and his own newly adopted two-year-old dog, Joey.

At this moment, the middle of July 2022, I was sleeping in late most days and working on this book and taking my dog on walks. It felt like my whole life was a weekend, or like I was always on vacation.

It's been almost three years since my accident. Much of that is blurry to me now but I know I lived it. I don't necessarily remember it, but I remember the main parts and major events that happened during that time.

The three-year anniversary is coming up, and by the time this book comes out it will have passed, but I was in the planning stages of a small gathering of all the coolest ladies I've met and loved throughout my life so far. This group of women are coming in from all over, from the whole Bay Area to San Diego.

I started volunteering with my first case manager. After leaving CNS, she had started an organization, Leona's Angels, named after her mom. They're trying to keep young adults out of a situation with houselessness and in houses. I ended up spending a lot of time in the car with her.

While she was driving us somewhere, she mentioned how my former physical therapist was convinced early on that she could get me to the point of unassisted walking. I had tried a walker once and a cane maybe three different times. I hated them and refused to learn to use them.

I texted Alex relaying the goal I heard she was committed to helping me reach. I told her I was now walking more than two and a half miles a day with Pepper. Many days, almost four. She texted me back saying how she always knew I could get to this point, and I had showed so much potential that I have lived up to.

I genuinely struggle with taking things slow. That is the feedback I've gotten from every physical therapist I've had since regaining consciousness. Slow down! I'm so go-go-go. It's frustrating.

My brain thinks faster than I can speak. My new post-injury brain is so tired of waiting for things to happen. I have to wait til my brain heals. Wait til someone can drive me where I need to go. Wait for Pepper to go to the bathroom. Wait til my aunt's mom is done in the bathroom. Just waiting. For other people. For myself.

> pepper's the answer
> i'm not sure to what questions
> def for the best eyes

chapter 25

september 7, 2022: my rebirthday

september seventh
it's become my rebirthday
a day to process

As I write this, it's been three years, and I fought so hard to get back pieces of my life. I wouldn't just accept what was expected of me. I wouldn't just be another scary statistic.

Never walking on my own again wasn't an option. Not being able to use my right hand anymore also was unacceptable.

I still want to do things. I still want to exist, survive, thrive. I want to live abroad. Fall in love. Adopt the cutest kids. I never wanted my life to end that fateful day that changed my life, possibly forever; probably forever.

I was planning on having a party to mark the one-year anniversary of my injuries and wanted to be surrounded by everyone who came to see me during my hospitalization.

Unfortunately, the coronavirus made it so I couldn't have the party I had envisioned. That sucked. I know the coronavirus affected everyone.

My ex was by my side throughout the beginnings of my injury. She was the only person I wanted to see. It so happens that her car ended up breaking down or something on that first year anniversary, making her presence impossible on my re-birthday.

The disappointment just sent me further down my spiral. I refused to see anyone. I wouldn't even let my dad come see me. I wasn't drinking regularly at that time in my life, but I had a few drinks that night.

My party had to get pushed back and back until, finally, September 7, 2021, two full years after my accident. It was worth the wait. By then, the guests had been vaccinated, but I still asked everyone to have a COVID test. It was outside in my aunt's backyard, so I didn't have to wear a mask the whole time, even though that had become the norm.

I invited so many people to celebrate with me. People from all walks of my life. My friends from college mingled with friends I made at the clinic. Friends of my mom's got to talk to three of my former roommates, who had flown in from far away to be with me that day.

Friends came from New Zealand, New York, Northern California, and Arizona. We had a vegetarian taco caterer and some vegan desserts from a bakery I found online.

I gave a speech at that party, between dinner and dessert. I expressed my deepest gratitude toward everyone, explaining how they helped me feel like a human during a dehumanizing part of my life. I focused on my aunt for her tireless dedication to my recovery.

Although they weren't there, I sang the praises of everyone who worked at CNS. I gave shoutouts to the staff of every hospital and residential home I was in.

It takes a certain type of person to want to go into a field that is so disheartening. I guess with patients like me who show tons of progress, it can be a job full of hope and joy.

There are patients, though, that I have seen first-hand, who don't seem to show progress or healing. It must be a depressing field, and they should be honored highly with praise. I am forever thankful to all of them.

The celebration was bittersweet. In an attempt to change the meaning of the day in my mind, my dear and talented friend Brooke tattooed a dandelion on my left thigh next to Teddy's face and the butterfly that had started as the heart my mom drew for me.

It was an intense and overwhelming day full of smiles, hugs, and tears. I think dandelions are the most resilient plants. They can bloom and emerge anywhere, in between cracks on the sidewalk. On fields. They're always popping up.

I wished there was a different reason I got to see almost all of my loved ones, but "it is, what it is," you know? Another way of looking at it, to reframe it in my mind, is everyone was there celebrating Teddy's life and my beating the odds.

Surrounded by smiles, I got to gather with the people in this world that I love the most and the ones who love me the most. Over time, I transformed something that marked the worst day in my life into a celebration. A day to be grateful for the life I got to continue living and to tell the people I love how much I love them.

My heart felt like it would explode. There was so much love. That morning, my aunt and I scattered some of Teddy's ashes on a birch tree in our front yard that we planted when my mom had closed her eyes for the last time. He will be with her for eternity in the dirt around her tree.

His ashes are also up in Arcata. His spirit will forever be in the redwoods and at the Arcata marsh, his favorite places to go in life. I have the last third of his ashes in a beautifully carved redwood box his vet sent me.

I hosted another party on September 7, 2022. I invited around nine girls to my little party/not dead yet celebration, only six could make it. There would be seven of us, including me.

Seven has always been a significant number in my life. Seven girls were at my party. My accident was on the seventh. I am pretty sure I was seven years old when my parents thought I had appendicitis.

This party was a competition potluck, something I had invented for my twenty-first birthday. No one wins but a winner is announced, encouraging people to bring their most exciting dishes. Whether that's an appetizer, a dessert, a main, or a drink. I've been a vegetarian since my freshman year of college, so the only rule is no meat, which means it ends up being mostly side dishes.

It will always be an incredibly hard day for me, but by inviting my closest friends, I transformed it into a day of love and gratitude. It reminds me that I could be dead, but I am not.

We mostly drank Prosecco. Only one friend drove herself to and from my house, and luckily, all the others were driven or were sleeping over. Once our evening officially started at 5:55, we started the festivities and had guava juice to make the most yummy and delicious mimosas out of Prosecco and guava juice.

I also made noodles because some couldn't bring a dish. They mostly brought dessert.

My worlds collided that day in the best way. It was a day filled with people from every single part of my life: my best friends since third grade hugged me with my college best friends, my friends from CNS—fellow young women also struggling with brain injuries—squeezed me throughout the day, reminding me how loved I was. Someone from every metaphorical pool I had swum in throughout my life were all in one place.

I know the day signifies something big for everyone who loves me. For a long time, it was hard to acknowledge that it affected anyone else but me. As I heal and process my trauma even further, I begin to understand and accept the impact it has had and will always have on me and the people closest to me.

My aunt had to get that horrible phone call everyone dreads getting about their loved ones. Diana then had to relay the news to everyone who needed to know. My friends had to get a terrible text or call informing them of my injuries and Teddy's demise. It has been so easy to be self-centered and only worry about myself for the past few years.

I'm slowly growing my awareness and getting better at empathy and compassion. Horrible things happen every day. All the time. There is no scale, no sadness greater or less than any other. If it hurts you, no one gets to tell you how you're feeling is wrong.

But I am making the best out of the worst things that have happened to me.

i'm telling you that
this world is open and full
it always gets good

chapter 26

what came next

unexpected change
no one warned me about it
came out of left field

Father's Day 2023, almost four years after my injury, I was biking with my dad when I unexpectedly swerved into loose gravel and fell. A friendly bystander helped me pick up my bike. Seconds after, I had no memory of the fall or the help.

We walked back to my house where I started violently seizing. My dad and roommate went into full save-Emily mode, and the paramedics arrived within minutes. I continued seizing in the ambulance.

When I arrived at the hospital, I was heavily sedated to put a stop to my seizures. My second MRI showed it wasn't a new injury that caused this, but rather the scarring left on my brain from my original injury almost four years before.

They kept me sedated for a day and a half to make sure the seizures stopped and so I would lay still in the MRI machine.

I was very confused to be back in the hospital. Shortly after my injury four years prior I had been taken to the closest ICU at Providence St. Joseph's in Eureka. In a morbidly ironic twist, I was taken to Providence St. Joseph's in Burbank after these seizures.

So, I was back in the same hospital gown I had been in before. Surrounded by walls painted the same color. Lying in the exact same type of ICU bed I had been in after my earlier trauma.

My neurologists explained to us that this sort of thing can happen, years can go by with no flare-ups until all of a sudden—BAM—a seizure, or in my case, multiple seizures. It was unexpected, but with the power of hindsight, there might've been some warnings.

My dog had been acting very strange and refusing to walk. I experienced a series of nighttime incontinence. I had been feeling especially unmotivated in the weeks before the seizures.

None of these things have a direct link to seizures, but they could have been signs. There is no way of knowing for sure that wetting the bed was me having mini seizures without a witness or a brain scan right after it happened.

I don't know how to describe my feelings about what happened. I felt scared, sad, and betrayed by my brain. I know there was nothing I could have done to prevent this, and I know I hadn't been living the healthiest lifestyle since leaving CNS.

Also, since moving out of Diana's, I was smoking too much weed. It was too easy for me to get and then consume, with multiple dispensaries within easy walking distance of my new apartment.

On the other hand, I had been trying to walk at least 10,000 steps a day for a few weeks before the seizures. I had been biking, going to the gym regularly at least twice a week, and cooking more than I had at my aunt's. But still, I should have been living healthier and putting more pressure on myself to care for myself.

I am still working on this book a lot, editing, but probably less than I should be. If there's a bright side, this was the wake-up call I needed before an angry, violent-sounding alarm shook up my life again.

Thankfully, I have experienced no negative setbacks after the seizures. Correlation doesn't always equal causation, but the only thing that seemed to change was my speech clearing up a lot post seizures.

I always had a slur after my accident. So much so that I've been accused of drinking when I have been stone-cold sober. I've even been refused drinks because they think I'm ALREADY DRUNK! Now I am the most hydrated girl at a party because I can't drink more than one alcoholic drink due to the anti-seizure meds I am taking.

I haven't found a way to use my environmental studies degree, and I can't work with little kids because I can't run after them. What I can do is write. It's always been something that came pretty easily to me, but it wasn't something I expected to do past my experience writing for my college newspaper. This career path found me.

I'm now typing this paragraph in February of 2024. Writing this book and the process of getting it edited and published has shown me a new path. From here on out, I am a published author with quite a few books to come.

I have a lot more to say.

raining all day long
be the brightness for someone
the sun through the clouds

about the author

EMILY SILVER OWEN is a first-time author and a vibrant survivor of a Traumatic Brain Injury. Her life's mission is to advocate for TBI awareness and to inspire others with her story of survival and resilience. Living in Studio City, CA, Emily continues to write and speak about  her experiences and participates in brain injury recovery groups, sharing her journey.

Emily's first children's book series focused on problems neurodivergent children might face is expected to be released in 2025. Emily's 2nd book, The Misadventures of a Brain Injured Twenty-Something is also in the works.

letter to caregivers

Dear Caregivers,

Caring for those we love is an immeasurable and profound expression of love. It's a journey marked by challenges, but isn't that the nature of all things truly worthwhile?

I still remember the shock and disbelief I felt when I received the call on the evening of September 7, 2019. An ER nurse informed me of a dreadful accident: Emily, who I call my niece, had been hit by a car. Hearing the words, "bleeding in the brain" and "life-threatening" shook me to my core.

In those moments, time seemed to stand still. I felt a surreal detachment, as though I was watching myself from afar, mechanically informing family and friends, packing, and arranging care for my mother. The reality of what had happened hadn't fully sunk in yet.

The drive from Los Angeles to Eureka was a blur of anxiety and fear. I found myself grappling with so many emotions, trying to brace for what awaited me. When I finally saw Emily in the ICU, connected to a myriad of machines, a mix of relief and heartache washed over me. Despite her peaceful appearance, her stillness was devastating—it was as if a part of her had already slipped away.

Standing by her bedside, I whispered a silent plea to her mother, "You can't take her, we aren't done with her yet." The uncertainty of not knowing when or if she would wake up, or to what extent she would recover was hard to bear.

It was during this time that I found strength in the memory of a former student, a young boy who had undergone brain surgery. His journey from being unable to move or speak to a chatty, bright child was a beacon of hope. It was a testament to the resilience of youth and the miraculous ability of the brain to heal.

As Emily's primary caregiver, I was thrust into a whirlwind of learning and decision-making. From the ICU to various rehabilitation centers, each day was a test of endurance and love. Family and friends rallied around Emily, ensuring she was never alone. Witnessing the slightest responses from her, like a simple smile or an attempt to mimic a kiss, filled me with a mix of joy and longing.

The journey was not without its challenges. The strain of managing Emily's recovery while caring for my mother weighed heavily on me. Emily's frustration and resentment were palpable, and I often found myself the target of her anger. It was a constant struggle to remind myself that her reactions were a natural part of her healing process.

But amidst the turmoil, there were moments of triumph. Seeing Emily take her first steps, despite the pain, brought tears of joy and pride. It was a reminder of the incredible journey we were on together.

Bringing Emily home was a turning point. We were stepping into a new phase of recovery, filled with challenges and adjustments. Yet, in those moments, I realized how fortunate we were to have the ability to provide her with the care she needed.

This experience taught me the importance of asking for and accepting help. The support of friends and family was invaluable, not just in practical matters, but in keeping my spirits up and reminding me that I was not alone in this journey.

To all caregivers, remember: every small step forward is a victory. Recovery is a unique journey for each individual, but what matters most is the love and support you provide. Stay strong, have faith, and cherish every moment of progress.

This book is more than Emily's story; it's a tribute to the resilience of the human spirit and the power of love and per-severance. It's a reminder of the strength that resides within each of us, waiting to be discovered in times of trial.

Keep hope alive,
Diana Rivera

acknowledgments

I AM BEYOND GRATEFUL FOR EVERYONE WHO HAS PLAYED A ROLE in my recovery. It is so noble for a person to commit to helping heal other people. To want to spend their time helping others. Especially all the doctors, physical therapists, occupational therapists, and speech therapists.

They all needed to go to so many schools for many, many years to be in the position that they were in. Thankfully, there are people in this world who want to spend their whole lives doing that job. I'm sure they see people worse off than me. They still want to come back to work the next day.

There are infinite amounts of people I want to thank.

First, I want to send a huge thank you to everyone on Team Emily. You know who you are. Thanks for making me feel as close to a real person as possible, not just like a patient. I want to single out my dad, for the endless amount of time he spent with me. I like to think of him as the leader of Team Emily. Thank you all for trying to keep a smile on my face, for loving me through the pain, for giving up your time to sit with me, and for always bringing me snacks.

Another star on Team Emily, the one who brought the best snacks and eventually brought another dog into my life, was Linda. She was part of every important stage in my recovery and beyond. Even though not formally a member of Team Emily, I also want to give special thanks to Guillermina, my aunt's mom's caregiver, who helped Diana and me in so many ways.

Next, I'd like to give another huge thank you to Jill—my therapist before and after the accident. I was on the phone with her as soon as I could speak full sentences. We did telehealth visits over FaceTime before I could even hold the phone while at Texhoma. My mom found Jill for me when she first got sick because Jill was, at the time, headquartered in the middle of Arcata, just off the town's plaza.

She's seen me through it all. Broken bones, a lot of heartache, the eventual death of my mother, and this whole car accident experience. She's the only person who knows everything about me from the last five years. My memory is terrible at times, and hers is fantastic, so she filled me in on things I don't remember but had told her about in the past.

I have to make sure to mention and thank the people who happened to be the first on the scene. The ones who were with me before the ambulance got to me, which leads me to thanking those paramedics who were on call when I got hurt. You're doing life-saving work.

I also want to thank every doctor, neuro-optometrist, and rehab therapist I've worked with throughout my recovery. At St. Joseph's up in Eureka, down south at Barlow Respiratory Hospital in Van Nuys, Neuro Restorative in Northridge, and the Acute Rehab Unit at Northridge Hospital. Even the ones I couldn't remember from when I was sleeping for weeks in a near coma. Don't take it personally. It was just my brain taking its sweet time to heal fully.

A huge thank you also to Dr. Vespa at UCLA Neurosurgery for looking at my first brain scans and providing invaluable advice, to Dr. Marder and the team at UCLA Semel Institute for Neuroscience and Human Behavior for the opportunity to participate in a potential new application for TMS therapy, and to Dr. Mi for giving me the Botox shots that gave me back the use of my right arm and hand.

Another huge, huge thank you to all the amazing people at CNS, Centre for Neuro Skills in Los Angeles. I do simultaneously wish I'd never met any of y'all, but I am so thankful and confusingly happy that if I had to have to have a brain injury team, I'm happy it was you.

Especially the team that worked closely with me. I think you guys already know how endlessly grateful I am, but here's a written version of my gratitude. So, the biggest thank you yelled at the top of my lungs to my initial core team at CNS, Victoria, Alex, and Tina. Thank you for being so dedicated and never giving up on me.

All of my friends already know how thankful I am for the time they dedicated to me and for all their cheers from the sidelines. They encouraged me, listened to the successes, cried with me, and always brought a smile to my face. A special shout out to the main characters—Xenia, Shanti, Julie, Brooke, and Zoe.

Special thank you's to my dad and Diana for proofreading my first draft and making sure everything I wrote was accurate. Thank you to Julie and to Diana's friend Pat for proofreading this whole thing once it was done. Thank you to Victoria for taking time out of your busy schedule to write the foreword. It meant a lot to me.

There are three people who were so integral to this book, it never would've gotten finished without them. One of them is my editor, Heather Asiyanbi. My ideas flow very easily, but the process of reorganizing and recognizing repetition is next to impossible for me since my injury. Heather was able to keep my voice present and my thoughts intact while making it so much more cohesive.

Next is Naja Hayward of Rainmaker Publishing. Diana and I looked at so many other options to help along this faster path of self-publishing. She is the best of the best. She has streamlined a confusing and usually difficult process into something enjoyable and frankly fun! I am forever indebted to her.

Last, but first in my heart, is Diana Rivera, my fairy godmother. Everything I need done, she makes it happen with such ease. She pushed me when I needed to be pushed and has stood strongly by my side since day one.

organizations near and dear to my heart

If you feel inspired to contribute, here are some causes that are dear to me:

- ASPCA
Support animals we love (and ones we don't know) and their welfare by visiting [aspca.org](https://www.aspca.org)

- World Central Kitchen
Help provide food and meals in the wake of disasters at donate.wck.org

- Pancreatic Cancer Action Network (PanCAN)
Please help further the fight against pancreatic cancer by donating at pancan.org

resources

Adaptive utensils

Amazon (of course) has a huge list of adaptive utensils, and they're good for kids or the elderly or young people with brain injuries. https://www.amazon.com/adaptive-utensils/s?k=adaptive+utensils

AFO (ankle foot orthotic)

I tried to find a simple explanation for mine, but AFO's come in all kinds of shapes and sizes, depending on what kind is needed and who will be wearing it. Basically, if you need one, your AFO will be for you, like mine were specific for me. You can read more about the positive benefits of using them here: https://www.ncbi.nlm.nih.gov/pmc/articles/PMC8392067/

Angel MedFlight

This is a service offered nationwide, not just on the West Coast. Their website says they serve all 50 states and more than 40 countries. https://angelmedflight.com/

Anti-gravity treadmill

There are a number of anti-gravity treadmills available, depending on the hospital or therapy facility. It was originally patented by NASA (I learned something new!). I found this website that explains how anti-gravity treadmills help patients with a number of health issues. https://community.scireproject.com/topic/body-weight-supported-treadmill/

BITS (Bioness Integrated Therapy System)

The touch-screen is how some of my cognitive and motor skills were assessed and improved. BITS is used for people of all ages and for many reasons. https://bionessrehab.com/bits/

Botox

The shots I received made all the difference in recovering use of my right arm and hand. A number of studies have been done over the years proving its effectiveness. This paper is a little long and confusing, but you can find the results if you scroll down just a little, and that's all that really matters, right? https://www.ncbi.nlm.nih.gov/pmc/articles/PMC7472282/

CIMT (Constraint-Induced Movement Therapy)

To help improve the performance of my right hand and arm, my left arm was made mostly immobile. All kinds of patients benefit, even little kids or anyone with a brain injury, like me. I found this cool website from the UK to explain it: https://www.manchesterneurophysio.co.uk/adults/services/constraint-induced-movement-therapy/index.php

CogMod (CNS-developed therapy)
If you visit the CNS website (https://www.neuroskills.com/) you can find all the therapies they offer. I did most of them, and I can tell you, they work!

Dynasplints
Even though I low-key hated them, my Dynasplints really helped improve my right leg and especially my right arm. They even have devices for animals! https://dynasplint.com/

Hyperbaric chamber
Brains need oxygen, especially to heal, and this is a great way to help that happen. I found this video of a girl who also suffered a brain injury and how a hyperbaric chamber helped her. https://www.youtube.com/watch?v=_ktYf1Yot2g

LSVT (Lee Silverman's Voice Treatment)
I couldn't cover every single therapy or treatment in the book so didn't include it, but at CNS one of my OT's used the BIG version of LSVT to help me with my balance and mobility. It was developed for patients with Parkinson's Disease and other neurological conditions. The LSVT organization also trains therapists on how to use LSVT. https://www.lsvt-global.com/
If you'd like to read a study about its effectiveness with speech, you can find one at the National Institutes of Health. https://www.ncbi.nlm.nih.gov/pmc/articles/PMC8782619/

TMS (Transcranial Magnetic Stimulation) **and rTMS** (Repetitive Transcranial Magnetic Stimulation)

The type of TMS that was used for my treatment was rTMS, which is used to create changes in brain activity. It helped quiet the right side of my brain so the left side could get stronger. Below are a few articles that give you some basic info. The first one is the case study that was done about my treatment:

https://www.sciencedirect.com/science/article/pii/S2773021223000718?via%3Dihub

https://my.clevelandclinic.org/health/treatments/17827-transcranial-magnetic-stimulation-tms

https://www.sciencedirect.com/science/article/pii/S1877065715000792

Vision therapy

This article from a neuro optometrist explains what light therapy is and how it works to help improve vision in different ways for people (like me) who live with a brain injury. https://www.optometrists.org/vision-therapy/neuro-optometry/vision-and-brain-injuries/traumatic-brain-injury-and-neuro-optometry/light-a-form-of-therapy/

For more insights and updates on my journey, visit
(http://www.emwritesbooks.com).

Discover additional content, read my blog, and be the first
to learn about my new book launches.

emwritesbooks.com

www.ingramcontent.com/pod-product-compliance
Lightning Source LLC
Chambersburg PA
CBHW021714120626
46545CB00004B/1560